D0292375

STARTING WITH HOBBES

Continuum's *Starting with . . .* series offers clear, concise and accessible introductions to the key thinkers in philosophy. The books explore and illuminate the roots of each philosopher's work and ideas, leading readers to a thorough understanding of the key influences and philosophical foundations from which his or her thought developed. Ideal for first-year students starting out in philosophy, the series will serve as the ideal companion to study of this fascinating subject.

Available now:

Starting with Berkeley, Nick Jones

Starting with Derrida, Sean Gaston

Starting with Descartes, C. G. Prado

Starting with Nietzsche, Ullrich Haase

Starting with Rousseau, James Delaney

Forthcoming:

Starting with Hegel, Craig B. Matarrese

Starting with Heidegger, Thomas Greaves

Starting with Hume, Charlotte R. Brown and William Edward Morris

Starting with Kant, Andrew Ward

Starting with Kierkegaard, Patrick Sheil

Starting with Leibniz, Lloyd Strickland

Starting with Locke, Greg Forster

Starting with Merleau-Ponty, Katherine Morris

Starting with Mill, John R. Fitzpatrick

Starting with Sartre, Gail Linsenbard

Starting with Schopenhauer, Sandra Shapshay

Starting with Wittgenstein, Chon Tejedor

STARTING WITH HOBBES

GEORGE MACDONALD ROSS

continuum

Continuum International Publishing Group
The Tower Building   80 Maiden Lane
11 York Road   Suite 704
London SE1 7NX   New York, NY 10038

www.continuumbooks.com

British Library Cataloguing-in-Publication Data
A catalogue record for this book is available from the British Library.

ISBN: HB: 1-8470-6160-5
        978-1-8470-6160-7
      PB: 1-8470-6161-3
        978-1-8470-6161-4

Library of Congress Cataloging-in-Publication Data
MacDonald Ross, G. (George)
Starting with Hobbes/George MacDonald Ross.
p. cm.
ISBN 978-1-8470-6160-7 (hardback) – ISBN 978-1-8470-6161-4 (pbk.)
1. Hobbes, Thomas, 1588–1679. I. Title.

B1247.M33 2009
192–dc22

2009001160

Typeset by RefineCatch Limited, Bungay, Suffolk
Printed and bound in Great Britain by the
MPG Books Group

CONTENTS

CONTENTS

INTRODUCTION

Hobbes had a vision of his complete philosophy as a logically organized system. It would consist of three separate volumes: *On Body*, *On the Human Being* and *On the Citizen*. As it happens, he wrote *On the Citizen* first, and completed the other two volumes much later. In the present book, I shall outline Hobbes's philosophy in more or less the order he intended. After the first chapter, on Hobbes's life and works, I shall begin with his theory of knowledge, which underpins his whole philosophical system. I shall then consider his materialism, which is, not surprisingly, the main theme of *On Body*. Having established to his satisfaction that only material objects exist, Hobbes then gives a materialist account of human psychology. Finally, I cover Hobbes's explanation of how selfish but vulnerable humans come together to form a civil society. Hobbes's religion is a pervasive theme throughout his works, and I devote a separate chapter to it. In the final chapter, I say something about the influence of Hobbes's thought.

Hobbes did not write in a vacuum, but was engaged in debate with his contemporaries. He lived during one of the most exciting periods in Western thought, which saw the transition from an essentially mediaeval world view in philosophy and science to a modern one. Hobbes was one of the leaders of the modern revolution, and particularly in the early chapters of the book, I establish the contrast between Hobbes's theories and concepts, and those of the ancient and mediaeval philosophers whose world view he was overturning. In addition, I consider similarities and dissimilarities with his contemporary modernists, especially Descartes.

Rather than simply asserting what Hobbes's position is, I have preferred to let Hobbes speak for himself as far as possible. This policy has two advantages. First, it gives you, the reader, a sense of Hobbes's style of thinking and writing, as well as your learning about his opinions. Second, it provides evidence that Hobbes really did believe what I say he believed, and an indication of where you can read more about a particular topic.

However, there is a problem with this policy. I have had long experience of teaching Hobbes's philosophy to undergraduates at a university with high entry requirements, and it is clear to me that the large majority have had little or no experience of reading early seventeenth-century English – except, perhaps, some heavily annotated Shakespeare and possibly parts of the Bible. When confronted with Hobbes's English, they cannot understand much of it, and they are unwilling or unable to go through the time-consuming task of looking up unfamiliar words, or words that may (or may not) have changed their meaning, in a historical dictionary such as the second edition of the Oxford English Dictionary.

The extent of the problem was brought home to me in a response to a course evaluation questionnaire on a course I gave comparing the philosophies of Hobbes and Descartes, where the students had been given Hobbes's writings in the original, and Descartes' in a modern translation. When asked which of the two philosophers they preferred and why, one student said he preferred Descartes, and explained 'Why couldn't Hobbes write decent modern English like Descartes did?' I am sure the student concerned fully appreciated the irony of his question, and it was a graphic way of making the point that students are not going to appreciate a philosopher's thoughts if they cannot understand the language in which they were expressed. We do not expect students to read Descartes in seventeenth-century French, because fluency in French is not an entry requirement. But neither is fluency in seventeenth-century English an entry requirement, and the English language has changed very considerably in the intervening four centuries.

I therefore resolved to translate the required reading from Hobbes texts into modern English, so that there would be a level playing field between Descartes and Hobbes. This is not a straightforward matter, because there is considerable resistance among academics to translating the English of earlier philosophers into modern English. The sort of arguments raised against translation are as follows.

First, translation forces a particular interpretation on the original text, whereas the reader should be confronted with the indeterminacies of the original. This is true, but it is equally an argument for not reading foreign texts in translation. In the real world, if students are expected to read primary texts (as they should be), the texts must be presented to them in a language they can understand. The history of philosophy is not an exercise in linguistics, but in understanding and evaluating ideas and concepts, which should not be obscured by unnecessary linguistic problems.

Second, students should not be admitted to university unless they can read philosophy in seventeenth-century English. It would be wonderful if we could expect this, just as it would be wonderful if we could expect students to read Plato in Greek, or Cicero in Latin, as used to be the case until the nineteenth century. But it is not the case, and philosophy would virtually disappear as a university discipline if this were a requirement.

Third, Hobbes was a brilliant writer of English, and it is a shame if readers are presented with a pedestrian modern substitute. This is a fair point, but Hobbes's brilliance is lost if it is not understood, and philosophers are primarily concerned with his ideas, and not with his literary style.

In order to get round the fastidiousness of academics about translating Hobbes's English into modern English, I initially focussed on translating his Latin writings into modern English. It is an interesting fact that both Hobbes and Descartes wrote sometimes in Latin and sometimes in English or French. Nobody should object to Hobbes's Latin works being translated into the same modern English as Latin works by Descartes, such as his *Meditations* or his *Principles of Philosophy*. But even here there is a problem, in that most of Hobbes's Latin works such as *On Body* and *On the Citizen* were almost immediately translated into English, with doubtful claims that the translations had been authorized by Hobbes himself. Many books about Hobbes use these translations as if they were Hobbes's own words. This has the double disadvantage of taking a contemporary translation as authoritative, and of providing a text which is largely unintelligible to most readers. I can see no reason for not translating these works into modern English.

Hobbes's most famous work, *Leviathan*, presents a special problem. Although he started writing it in Latin, he finished it in English. Then, towards the end of his life, and in order to ensure his legacy outside the English-speaking world, he translated it into Latin. This raises the question of which is the definitive version. There is a case to be made that the later version is more definitive, as reflecting Hobbes's more mature position. It is also significant that the Latin version was printed in Amsterdam, out of the reach of the English censors, who disapproved of Hobbes's religious and political views. On the other hand, quite a lot of interesting material in the English version is dropped from the Latin, although the Latin version has appendices which are crucial for understanding Hobbes's religious views.

My policy has been to translate passages from Hobbes's Latin works into modern English as the default. Where he says things only in the English version, I translate them into modern English in exactly the same way as I would translate from Latin, French or any other language. Likewise, I quote from a number of works which were written in English without being translated into Latin, and again I translate them into modern English. I recognize that something is always lost in translation, and I hope that anyone who is starting with Hobbes by reading this book will continue with Hobbes by reading his works in the original.

Most of Hobbes's writings are divided into short, numbered sections. My references to these using Hobbes's own numbering are more precise than page references to any printed edition, and are equally valid for any edition. The main exception is *Leviathan*, where the chapters are quite long, and there is the added complication that I sometimes refer to the Latin version, and sometimes to the English version. It so happens that there is one reasonably priced edition which includes both the English text, and a translation of all the significant Latin variants. This is Edwin Curley (ed.), Thomas Hobbes, *Leviathan* (Indianapolis/Cambridge: Hackett, 1994). For ease of reference, I give page numbers to this edition, even though the actual wording in the present volume is my own translation of Hobbes's Latin and English.

i. ABBREVIATIONS

The only abbreviation I use is CL followed by a number, to refer to the page numbers in Curley's edition of *Leviathan* which correspond to my own translation.

CHAPTER 1

LIFE AND WORKS

i. EARLY YEARS

Thomas Hobbes was born on 5 April 1588, in the village of Westport, near Malmesbury, Wiltshire. At the time, there was widespread fear of the impending Spanish invasion, and Hobbes sometimes said that his cowardly nature was due to the fearfulness of his mother being transferred to her unborn son. His father was a poorly educated and incompetent vicar, who eventually abandoned his family, leaving Hobbes to be brought up by his uncle, Francis. Francis was a prosperous glover, who was wealthy enough to pay for Hobbes's education, and to leave him some rented farm land in his will.

Hobbes went to various local schools from the age of 4 to 14, when he left for Magdalen Hall, Oxford in 1602 or 1603. Although 14 was not an exceptionally early age to go to university in those days, he was one of the youngest of his cohort. But he was well prepared, and he was a good enough scholar to be able to present his last schoolteacher, Robert Latimer, with a translation of Euripides' *Medea* from Greek into Latin verse. At university, he would have studied a mixture of Aristotelian logic and philosophy, the classics of rhetoric, moral philosophy and history, and some mathematics and science. On his own account, he was not a very assiduous student, but his education was probably broader and more enlightened than he later recalled it as being. He finally graduated in 1608.

ii. THE CAVENDISH FAMILY

Later that year, on the recommendation of the Master of his college, he was appointed tutor to William Cavendish, and he was to spend most of the rest of his life with successive generations of the family. At this point, it will be useful to list who the relevant members of the family were, since, confusingly, they nearly all had the same name.

Bess of Hardwick (1527–1608) was the founder of the dynasty, and she died just when Hobbes was appointed. She acquired a huge fortune, partly by marrying a succession of four wealthy husbands who died and left their money to her, and partly through shrewd investment in land. She built stately homes at Chatsworth, Oldcotes, Worksop and Hardwick. The last was the most impressive, with more glass than wall on its front elevation. The second floor was dominated by a throne room for an anticipated visit by her friend Queen Elizabeth – but tragically the visit never took place.

There were two lines of succession through two sons of her second husband, William Cavendish (c. 1505–1557). On the one side, there was William Cavendish (1551–1626), who inherited Hardwick, and then Chatsworth after the death of his elder brother in 1616. He became a baron in 1605, and the first earl of Devonshire in 1618. His son William (1590–1628), Hobbes's first tutee, became the second earl. This William also had a son called William (1617–1684), who was also Hobbes's tutee, and who became the third earl. Finally, the third earl had a son, again a William (1641–1707), who became the fourth earl, and in 1694, the first duke of Devonshire.

The other line of succession was through Charles Cavendish (1553–1617), who bought Welbeck Abbey in Nottinghamshire, and Bolsover Castle, next to Hardwick. His son, yet another William Cavendish (1593–1676), was created earl of Newcastle-upon-Tyne in 1628, and was one of Hobbes's most important patrons.

iii. TUTOR TO THE SECOND EARL OF DEVONSHIRE

William, the future second earl, specifically requested a young tutor, so that he would be a friend and companion as well as a teacher.

In fact Hobbes was just 2 years older. It is unknown how much Hobbes taught William, but he later reminisced that these were the happiest years of his life. They spent a lot of time hunting and hawking together, and Hobbes was responsible for William's money – a duty which included asking people for loans to cover his extravagant lifestyle. From June 1614 to October 1615 they went on a tour to Rome, Naples and Venice, and both became fluent in Italian. When in Venice, they made the acquaintance of the philosopher Pietro Sarpi (1552–1623) and his assistant Fulgenzio Micanzio, with whom William maintained a correspondence until his death in 1628. Hobbes translated Micanzio's letters from Italian into English so that they could have a wider circulation. In 1620, William published an anonymous book called *Horae subsecivae* (Hours at Leisure), consisting of an account of their stay in Rome, and miscellaneous essays and discourses. It may be that three of the discourses were written by Hobbes.

Around this time, Hobbes did some work for Francis Bacon (1561–1626), the philosopher and Lord Chancellor, writing down his thoughts while he walked in his park, and translating some of his essays into Latin.

In the early 1620s, the second earl gave Hobbes shares in two colonial companies, the Virginia Company and the Somers Islands Company. He attended many of their management meetings, and he had the opportunity to become acquainted with a range of prominent people. He was becoming increasingly known as a well networked intellectual.

In August 1627, Hobbes, William and the poet Dr Richard Andrews went on a tour of the Derbyshire Peak District, visiting the best known tourist attractions (called 'the wonders of the Peak'). Both Andrews and Hobbes wrote poems about the trip: Andrews in English and Hobbes in Latin. Hobbes's poem was printed soon afterwards with the title *De mirabilibus pecci*. It was reprinted a number of times, and an edition of 1678 included an English translation with the title *The wonders of the peak in Darby-shire, commonly called the Devil's Arse of Peak*. Hobbes was a keen walker, and he would go for a walk every day (in wet weather he would walk up and down the long gallery of Hardwick).

So, as to take a note of any thoughts he might have while walking, he had a walking stick made with an inkwell in the handle.

Around the same time, Hobbes produced a far more significant work. This was a translation of Thucydides's *History of the Peloponnesian War*, and he was the first person to translate it into English directly from the Greek. Thucydides was his favourite historian, probably because of his Hobbes-like dispassionate and incisive analysis of political realities. For no obvious reason, he delayed having the translation published, until he finally took action in 1628, on the occasion of the premature death of his patron, the second earl. He wrote a dedication to the young third earl, aged 12, praising his father, hoping that this would earn him continued employment. The book was published in 1629, but he was not re-employed (though he still received an allowance).

iv. TUTOR TO GERVASE CLIFTON

Hobbes spent most of 1629 and 1630 employed by Sir Gervase Clifton, taking his son Gervase on a European tour. They went to Paris, Geneva and Orléans. It was in Geneva that Hobbes underwent an intellectual revolution. Although he had studied some geometry at school and university, it never particularly interested him. But, now he happened to pick up a copy of Euclid's *Elements*, and opened it at proposition 47 of Book 1. As he traced the proof back through earlier demonstrations, he became fascinated by the way that complex truths could be derived with absolute certainty from a few simple definitions and axioms. This not only stimulated much deeper study of geometry, but also had a profound influence on his theory of knowledge, which was modelled on geometry. He later claimed that it was in about 1630 that he started developing his ideas about perception and optics, and first expounded them to the earl of Newcastle and other scientist/philosophers such as Newcastle's brother Charles, Newcastle's chaplain Robert Payne and Walter Warner.

v. TUTOR TO THE THIRD EARL OF DEVONSHIRE

On returning to Hardwick in November 1630, Hobbes was re-employed by the countess of Devonshire to tutor her elder son, William, the third earl. In 1634, Hobbes and William spent the summer in Oxford and Malmesbury, and then went on to Paris, where they stayed until August 1635. They planned to travel to Venice, but they may not have got there. They were certainly in Rome by December, and it seems likely that en route they visited Galileo Galilei (1564–1642) in his villa near Florence. In May they returned to Paris *via* Turin, Geneva and Lyons, and first made the acquaintance of Marin Mersenne (1588–1648), who was one of the leading lights of the new philosophy in France. Hobbes and William went back to England in October 1636.

For the next few years, Hobbes was in a frenzy of creativity, developing original ideas in mathematics, science, philosophy, logic, psychology and politics, and bringing them together into a systematic whole. However, the only work he completed during this period was a short Latin work on optics (the *optical Treatise*), which was published in a collected volume by Mersenne in 1644. He was probably goaded into writing by receiving, in 1637, a copy of the *Discourse on the Method* by René Descartes (1596–1650), which included his *Dioptrics*. Hobbes was very concerned to be recognized for the originality of his own ideas, and he was being upstaged by his younger contemporary, who was later to accuse him of plagiarism. In fact, apart from a major disagreement as to whether immaterial substances existed or not, their accounts of the material world and the human body were quite similar. So, Hobbes had a psychological motivation to distance himself as far as possible from Descartes. In 1640, he wrote a 56-page letter to Mersenne criticizing the *Discourse*; but unfortunately it has not survived.

This was the time when Hobbes conceived his grandiose vision of a three-part *Elements of Philosophy*, in which everything would be proved scientifically, following the model set by Euclid. The first part, *On Body* (*De corpore*), would cover metaphysics and physics, and establish that all physical phenomena can be explained on the principle that nothing exists except matter in motion. The second part, *On the Human Being* (*De homine*), would show that all human behaviour can be explained on the same terms. The third part, *On the Citizen* (*De cive*), would give a scientific account of the origins of civil society, and argue for a single sovereign power with absolute authority. Although Hobbes eventually completed his plan, the parts were written and published in the wrong order, and many other publications intervened.

vi. EXILE IN PARIS

In 1640, at the instigation of the earl of Newcastle, Hobbes wrote a summary of most of his whole scheme in English, with the title *The Elements of Law*. It was initially distributed only in manuscript, but later it was printed, without Hobbes's permission, in two parts in 1650 and 1651. Ironically, it lacked the most foundational element, which was the metaphysics and physics (later to be covered in *On Body*). However, his defence of the absolute authority of the king in the political part of the work made him many enemies at a time when civil war was about to break out, and he emigrated to Paris. His tutoring of William had ceased, because William had come of age, and Hobbes had accumulated enough savings (£500) to last him many years in exile. In fact he stayed away for 11 years.

Hobbes re-established contact with Mersenne, who held regular meetings of intellectuals, including individuals such as the anti-Aristotelian philosopher Pierre Gassendi (1592–1655), and English fellow exiles such as the pirate turned philosopher Sir Kenelm Digby (1603–1665), and the Catholic philosopher Thomas White (1593–1676). Mersenne was a staunch ally of Descartes, and he arranged for the manuscript of his *Meditations on First Philosophy* to be distributed to a number of noteworthy philosophers, so that it could be published with their (anonymous) objections and Descartes' replies. It was duly published in 1641, and the third set of objections was supplied by Hobbes – the first of his philosophical writings to appear in print. The exchange was bad-tempered on both sides, and neither seemed to appreciate the position of the other. There is no clear evidence whether they ever met in person; but if they did, the encounter was unlikely to have been an easy one.

The following year, in 1642, Mersenne gave Hobbes's philosophical career a further boost by arranging for the private printing of Hobbes's *On the Citizen*, which was the third part of his *Elements of Philosophy*, but the first to be written and published. It had a far wider readership when it was reprinted in Holland in 1647, and it did much to establish Hobbes's international reputation. It was probably also at Mersenne's suggestion that Hobbes wrote a long treatise criticizing the recently published *Three Dialogues about the World* (1642) by Thomas White. White's work covered a wide range of questions in physics, metaphysics and theology in a way which combined some of the ideas of the new philosophy with much traditional scholasticism. Hobbes's criticisms are mainly directed towards his scholasticism, and some of his theological assumptions. Despite the immense amount of work that Hobbes put into his critique, the manuscript may have been read by no-one other than Mersenne (who wrote some marginal comments on it). It disappeared until it was rediscovered and published in the twentieth century. One other piece by Hobbes that Mersenne published in 1644 was a brief summary of Hobbes's philosophy, forming a preface to a book by Mersenne called *Ballistics* (the science of projectiles).

After completing the criticism of White, Hobbes tried to concentrate on writing the first part of the *Elements of Philosophy, On Body* – but he was destined to suffer many interruptions. In April 1645, the earl of Newcastle fled to Paris with his brother Charles after losing the battle of Marston Moor. Soon after his arrival, he prevailed upon Hobbes and the exiled Anglican bishop of Derry, John Bramhall (1594–1663), to conduct a debate on the freedom of the will. Hobbes wrote up an account of his side of the argument in a treatise called *Of Libertie and Necessitie*, which was published, without his permission, in 1654. That publication was followed by a number of other publications in which Hobbes pursued his argument with Bramhall in sometimes tedious detail.

In 1645, Hobbes returned to writing *On Body*, but he soon suffered three further interruptions. In the summer of 1646, he was appointed to teach mathematics to Prince Charles, the future Charles II, who had just arrived in Paris. This turned out to be an important appointment, because he had valuable patronage from the King after the restoration. The second interruption was in the latter part of 1647, when Hobbes suffered a serious illness from which he nearly died, and which kept him in bed for 6 months. One good thing to come of his illness was that later, when accused of atheism, he was in a position to point out that he had summoned an Anglican clergyman to administer the last rites.

The third interruption was Hobbes's decision to write an entirely different book, namely *Leviathan*. *Leviathan* can be regarded as an expanded version of the *Elements of Law*. It is written in English, and it starts with chapters on metaphysics, logic and psychology, before moving on to political philosophy, which constitutes the bulk of the work. However, there is much more that is relevant primarily to the English situation at a time of civil war, whereas the *Elements of Law* and the *Elements of Philosophy* were conceived as universally and timelessly true. It is clear that Hobbes felt a need to address his fellow citizens at just the time when England seemed to be reverting to the very state of nature his philosophy was designed to avoid. It is unclear when Hobbes started work on *Leviathan* (it could have been any time between 1646 and 1649), but it was ready for publication, in England, in 1651. The fact that it was published in England, and just before he returned home, is strong evidence that he did not see it as a work which would get him into serious trouble, whether for his royalism (given that Charles I was executed only in 1649), or for his unorthodox religious views. *Leviathan* supported any sovereign power which could protect its people, whether the Commonwealth of Cromwell or a Stuart king, and Hobbes presented Charles with a special manuscript copy of *Leviathan* just before leaving Paris.

There is a difference of opinion among commentators as to whether Hobbes started writing Leviathan in Latin, and only later decided to make it an English work, or whether he wrote it in English from the start. Hobbes's own testimony in his verse autobiography suggests the former. Either way, in his old age he wanted to establish his reputation for posterity, and he prepared a two-volume edition of his Latin writings, which was published in Amsterdam in 1668, and reprinted (with some corrections by Hobbes) in 1670. Latin was still the *lingua franca* of intellectuals, and few people outside the British Isles could read English. Hobbes was sufficiently proud of *Leviathan* to include a Latin version of it in this edition. The Latin version is not a straight translation, but omits some things which were either special to the English situation, or were witticisms untranslatable into Latin. On the other hand, it includes three appendices which justify Hobbes's religious views to an extent not equalled in any of his other writings.

vii. RETURN TO ENGLAND

By 1651, life in Paris had fewer attractions for Hobbes, especially since the death of Mersenne in 1648. Royalists such as the earl of Devonshire had been able to return as early as 1645 by compromising with parliament in order to preserve their estates. Now that his historically most significant work had been published, Hobbes decided to go back home. One of his motives was that French Catholics took badly to *Leviathan*, and he was frightened that he would be arrested. He left in December, and returned to stay with the Devonshires.

In the 1650s he lived mostly in London, studying and writing. He completed the Latin *On Body*, which was published in 1655. An anonymous English translation appeared in 1656. It claimed to have been approved by Hobbes, and some passages are significantly different from the original. Strangely, however, when *On Body* was reprinted in the 1668 edition of his Latin works, it did not include the changes made in the English translation. The much shorter *On the Human Being* was published in 1658, and the trilogy of the *Elements of Philosophy* was finally complete when Hobbes was 70.

Hobbes's political and theological views and his hostility towards universities gained him many enemies. This was probably the main reason why he was never invited to join the Royal Society, despite being one of the most illustrious proponents of the new science. However, it also has to be said that Hobbes rejected the empiricism of the Royal Society's mission, and his confidence in the power of reason would not have gone down well with its members. Hobbes attributed his success in producing original theories to the fact that he relied on reasoning alone, and not on books, tradition or university teaching. As John Aubrey says in his *Brief Life of Thomas Hobbes*: 'He was wont to say that if he had read as much as other men, he should have known no more than other men' (p. 157).

Even if the main motive for attacking Hobbes was religious or political, he certainly laid himself open to criticism for some of his mathematical and scientific views – in particular his belief that he had succeeded in squaring the circle, and his denial of a vacuum. The latter led to an argument with Robert Boyle (1627–1691) over Boyle's experiments with a vacuum pump. Hobbes's attempt to square the circle inspired a refutation by John Wallis (1616–1703), one of the most significant mathematicians of his time, in his *Examination of Hobbes's Geometry* (1655). Hobbes replied in a succession of books: *Six Lessons to the Professors of the Mathematicks . . . at the University of Oxford* (1656), *On the Principles and Reasoning of Geometers* (1672), *A Geometrical Rose Garden* (1671) and *Mathematical Light* (1672). The trouble was that Hobbes only started studying mathematics in middle age, and he was self-taught. He had no difficulty with the idea that professional mathematicians might be wrong, since everybody had been wrong in other branches of knowledge such as scholastic philosophy and political theory. But while his amateurish self-confidence was in some ways an asset in philosophy and politics, it was just embarrassing in mathematics. When he was at Oxford, it may well have been the case that there was little knowledge of mathematics that advanced much beyond what was known in antiquity. But great strides had been made during Hobbes's lifetime, and by his old age he was seriously out of touch. His obstinacy in clinging to mathematical beliefs that were plain wrong did much to harm his reputation as one of the leading thinkers of his day.

viii. LAST YEARS

A few days after the restoration in 1660, the king saw Hobbes while riding in the royal coach along the Strand, and kindly doffed his hat to him as his former mathematics tutor. A week later, Aubrey arranged for Hobbes to have an audience with the king while he was sitting for a portrait by Samuel Cooper (who later painted a watercolour miniature of Hobbes). The king so enjoyed the conversation that he gave orders for Hobbes to have free access to him. Some time later, he granted him a pension of £105 a year (though it was not in fact always paid). When he was at court, the wits would often tease him. The king nicknamed him 'the bear', and he would say 'Here comes the bear to be baited' (Aubrey, p. 154).

Hobbes was fortunate to have the protection of the king, as well as of the Cavendish family and other powerful friends, because the leaders of the Anglican church were very hostile towards his views. In 1662, parliament passed a Printing Act, which made it impossible for Hobbes to publish anything controversial about religion or politics. This is no doubt one reason why he had his collected Latin works published in Amsterdam (the other reason being that they were directed more towards an international than to an English public). In the early 1660s there were rumours that some bishops were planning to prosecute him for heresy, and in 1666, a House of Commons committee was empowered to 'receive Informacion toucheing such bookes as tend to Atheisme Blasphemy or Prophanenesse or against the Essence or Attributes of God. And in perticular ... the booke of Mr Hobbs called the Leuiathan' (quoted in Malcolm 1996, pp. 35–36). Nothing seems to have come of it, but Hobbes was panicked into burning some papers which might have been incriminating, and this may be why there is so little about the nature of God and the immortality of the soul in his writings. He also wrote a treatise on the law of heresy, in which he argued that no-one should be put to the stake for it, and he defended himself from the accusation of heresy in chapter 2 of the appendix to the Latin *Leviathan*.

Hobbes was remarkably prolific in his last years. In addition to works already mentioned (his mathematical writings, his debate with Bishop Bramhall, and the translation of *Leviathan* into Latin), he wrote the following: *Problems in Physics* (1662); *Ten Days of Physics* or *Ten Dialogues of Natural Philosophy* (1668); a dialogue on the history of the civil war, published without permission in 1679, and later known as *Behemoth; A Dialogue between a Phylosopher and a Student, of the Common-Laws of England*; a Latin poem called *Ecclesiastical History* (completed in 1671, published in 1688);

an autobiography in Latin verse (written in 1672) and translations of the whole of Homer's Odyssey, and then of the Iliad (published between 1673 and 1676).

Hobbes enjoyed good health for most of his life, apart from three serious illnesses in France and London, and a shaking of the hand which began to affect him in his 60s, and eventually prevented him from writing, so that he had to dictate to a scribe. For the last year or so, even that became increasingly difficult. In October 1679, he began to suffer from a pain when urinating. In the middle of November, the Devonshire family made its annual move from Chatsworth to the warmer climate of Hardwick, and Hobbes insisted on coming with them. He arrived safely, but on 27 November he had a stroke, which paralysed him and prevented him from speaking. He died a week later, on 4 December, and he was buried in the nearby church of Ault Hucknall.

He had joked that he wanted his gravestone to read 'This is the true philosopher's stone', punning on his rejection of alchemy and other such superstitions. Instead it read, modestly and prosaically, 'Buried here are the bones of Thomas Hobbes of Malmesbury, who for many years served two earls of Devonshire, father and son. He was an honourable man, and well known for the fame of his learning at home and abroad. He died on the 4th of December 1679, at the age of 91.'

CHAPTER 2

THEORY OF KNOWLEDGE

i. MEDIEVAL THEORIES OF PERCEPTION

During the middle ages, philosophers believed that we see things because very thin surfaces of objects, called 'species', travel through the air, enter our eyes and come into contact with the quasi-material 'animal spirits' in our heads. Some also held that they are then emitted through the eyes again, and towards the object they came from. This account has two great strengths. First, it explains why we see things as external to us, whereas modern theories hold that the process of perception ends in the brain, without necessarily explaining how we project visual images outwards. You might expect visual images to be perceived as being inside the head, just as we hear music as inside our heads when listening through headphones.

The second strength of this account is that it accords with our commonsense belief that things really are as they appear to us, and that we all, by and large, see things the same way. For example, the colours we see in an object really are in the object itself, even when no one is looking at it or when it is in the dark, because the species we perceive were once the actual surface of the object.

There were, however, serious difficulties with the theory, which medieval philosophers devoted an immense amount of intellectual effort to resolving. To give just a few examples:

• While the theory has some initial appeal in the case of vision, it seems much less plausible in the case of the other senses. Does

it even make any sense to say that taste operates through gusta-
tory species, or touch through tactile species?

- How can species cross each others' paths without destroying
each other? (This is also a problem if you believe that vision is
caused by tiny particles travelling at the speed of light.)
- Why do species get smaller the further you are away from an
object?
- If species are constantly leaving the surfaces of things, why
don't objects evaporate?
- Why can we not see things in the dark?

ii. GALILEO'S THEORY OF PERCEPTION

The first person to abandon this whole approach was Galileo. In a
tantalizingly brief passage in his book *The Assayer*, which was
published in 1623, he makes a distinction between what were later
known as primary and secondary qualities. Primary qualities are
those which inhere in the object itself, whereas secondary qualities
exist only in the mind of the observer, and are caused by the operation of the primary qualities on the sense organs. If there were
no sentient beings, there would be no secondary qualities. Here is
Galileo's list of primary qualities:

> I say that, as soon as I conceive of a piece of matter, or a
> corporeal substance, I feel myself necessarily compelled to con-
> ceive along with it, that it is bounded, and has this or that shape;
> that in relation to some other body it is either small or large; that
> it is in this or that place, and in this or that time; that it is in
> motion or at rest; that it either touches or does not touch some
> other body; and that it is one, few, or many (*The Assayer*, pp.
> 196–97).

All other qualities are secondary and only in the mind: colours,
sounds, warmth, smells and so on. Colours and sounds are caused
by vibrations in the air started by the perceived object and picked
up by the eyes and ears, and smells are caused by material particles
wafting through the air and landing in the nose.

There is one serious inadequacy in Galileo's account, in that he overlooks something which was already known in antiquity, in particular by the Stoic school of philosophy. This is that the properties of a material object must include something which distinguishes it from empty space of the same size and shape – something which makes it substantial as contrasted with absence of being. So, the Stoics defined matter as extension (i.e. its geometrical properties) combined with 'antitypy', or resistance to penetration and acceleration. If you push against a volume of empty space, it offers no resistance. But if you push against a physical object, you need to exert a force to get inside it or to set it in motion. Despite this inadequacy, which philosophers and physicists gradually addressed during the rest of the seventeenth century, it is difficult to overestimate the significance of Galileo's insight. He opened the way to a radical dualism between the subjective world of experience, known through the qualitative characteristics of colours, sounds, feelings and so on, and the objective world of scientific truth, described in the language of mathematics. As Galileo put it in *The Assayer*, p. 25:

> Philosophy is written in this vast book, which continuously lies open before our eyes (I mean the universe). But it cannot be understood unless you have first learned to understand the language and recognize the characters in which it is written. It is written in the language of mathematics, and the characters are triangles, circles, and other geometrical figures. Without such means, it is impossible for us humans to understand a word of it, and to be without them is to wander around in vain through a dark labyrinth . . .

Later philosophers such as Berkeley (1685–1753), Hume (1711–1776) and Kant (1724–1804) would reject this radical dualism, and maintain that science is about the world of experience shared by all human beings, and not about some separate, more objective world, known only to scientists. Nevertheless, Galileo's dualism was hugely influential, and probably represents the majority view of practising scientists today. There is a good case for saying that 1623 was the year in which modern philosophy and science were born, since it is also the year in which Francis Bacon published his *Increase of the Sciences*, a seminal text arguing for the empirical method in science.

iii. DESCARTES' THEORY OF PERCEPTION

Descartes was the first major philosopher to follow Galileo's distinction between primary and secondary qualities. In his *The World, or Treatise on Light*, written around 1633, but not published until after his death, he uses the same example as Galileo's of the sensation of tickling being only in the subject and not in the object. In later writings, he comes out with much the same distinction between primary and secondary qualities as Galileo, and he too fails to make any distinction between a physical object and an equal volume of empty space. Indeed, he explicitly defines matter as extension and nothing more, which logically excludes any distinction between matter and the extension it occupies.

Descartes' main difference from Galileo is that he distinguishes between primary qualities as we perceive them, which are as subjective as secondary qualities, and primary qualities as they are known by reason, which are objective. Thus, in the *Meditations* 3, p. 39, he distinguishes between two different ideas of the sun:

> I find in myself two ideas of the sun. One is derived from the senses, . . . and it makes the sun appear to me to be very small. The other is derived from astronomical reasoning (i.e. obtained from certain innate ideas . . .), and it shows the sun to be many times larger than the earth.

Few subsequent philosophers were willing to follow Descartes in attributing our scientific knowledge of a real world underlying the illusory world of experience to innate ideas given to us by God. Nevertheless, he implicitly issued a stark challenge: if you want to say that the real world is different from how it appears to you, what grounds do you have? It would be paradoxical to say that experience teaches us that the real world is unlike how we experience it. The scientific consensus is that the real world is indeed very different from the world of experience, and one of the big issues of modern philosophy is to explain how science can tell us about the nature of reality, when all our knowledge is ultimately derived from experience, and God is excluded as a source of knowledge. Hobbes's philosophy is an attempt to rise to this challenge.

iv. HOBBES'S THEORY OF PERCEPTION

Hobbes first disseminated his views on the distinction between primary and secondary qualities, or between the world of appearance and the world of reality, in his *Elements of Law*, of 1640. Although he was jealous of his own priority in this discovery, it is quite likely that he was influenced by his discussions with leading philosophers on the continent (including Galileo himself in 1635), and his reading of the latest books. However, his arguments are original, and he is commendable for considering all the senses, whereas later philosophers often made the mistake of thinking only in terms of the sense of sight. In *On Body* chapter 25 section 10 he runs through all the senses, and In the *Elements of Law* chapter 2 section 4, in addition to visual examples of the subjectivity of our sensory images, Hobbes includes sounds:

> Because, in vision, the image consisting of colour and shape is the knowledge we have of the qualities of the object of that sensation, it is very easy to fall into the opinion that the said colour and shape are the actual qualities themselves. For the same reason, it is easy to think that sound and noise are the qualities of a bell, or of the air. This opinion has been accepted for so long, that its denial must seem to fly in the face of common sense. On the other hand, the opinion can only be maintained on the assumption that there are visible and intelligible species, which travel to and from the object; and this is worse than non-commonsensical, since it is obviously impossible.

This passage is remarkable for making it clear that Hobbes expects his readers to be *surprised* by his claim that the qualities we perceive in objects are not in the objects themselves, but in the mind of the observer. In the *Elements of Law* chapter 2 sections 5–9, he uses a number of arguments in support of his position.

- When we look at something in a mirror, the image is not in the object, because we see it as behind the mirror, which is not where the object is.
- Under certain conditions we see double. It is impossible for both images to be in the object; and since we have no grounds for saying which is in the object, it follows that neither is in the object.
- If we are punched in the eye, we see a flash of light without there being any external object corresponding to the light. So generally, the sensation of light is caused by motions acting on the eye and the optic nerve, and the sensation is nothing other than a motion in the brain.
- The same is true of other senses. For example, echoes show that sounds are not in the objects that cause them, because they come from different places. There are only motions, such as the motion of the clapper in a bell, the motion of particles of air and motion of the nerves and the brain. It is only at the last stage that we are conscious of sound as we know it. Again, smell and taste are different for different people, so they are in the person and not in the object; and sensations such as that of warmth are in us, and not in the fire that warms us.

In short, Hobbes rejects the commonsense view that makes no distinction between perceptual images in the mind and external objects of perception. As he puts it in *Leviathan* chapter 1 (CL 7):

> And although . . . the genuine object itself sometimes seems to be clothed in its image, it is always the case that the object itself is one thing, and the image of the object another.

In the English version of the same chapter (CL 7), he ridicules the scholastic theory of perception taught in the universities in a way utterly characteristic of Hobbes at his wittiest and most scathing:

But philosophy faculties in all the universities of Christendom, relying on certain texts of Aristotle, teach another doctrine. They say that the cause of vision is that the thing seen emits in every direction a visible species, or (in English) a visible show, apparition, or aspect, or a being seen; and seeing occurs when it enters the eye. And they say that the cause of hearing is that the thing heard emits an audible species, that is, an audible aspect, or audible being seen; and hearing occurs when it enters the ear. They even say that the cause of understanding is that the thing understood emits an intelligible species, that is, an intelligible being seen, which makes us understand by coming into our understanding. This is not an argument for abolishing universities altogether. But because I am later going to talk about their function in society, I must let you see what things need to be corrected in them whenever the occasion arises. The frequency of meaningless language is one.

Hobbes replaces the scholastic account with his own theory of perception, which has much in common with the theories of Galileo, Descartes and other early modern philosophers, but also has its own distinctive features which remained highly influential throughout the seventeenth century. The main focus is on vision, because the other senses seemed relatively unproblematic. Hobbes's task was to explain how we can have perceptions of light and colour from distant objects, when all that exists is matter in motion, and the only effect one object can have on another is to set it in motion. It just seemed obvious that coming into direct contact with an object through touch sets up a motion in the nerves; that sound consists of vibrations in the air which set up corresponding vibrations in the eardrum and nerves; and that taste and smell involve direct contact with volatile particles in the mouth and nose. Vision was more mysterious.

v. THE NATURE OF LIGHT

As we shall see later, Hobbes held that nothing exists except matter in motion, and that the only way that one body can act upon another is by pushing against it, whether directly, or indirectly through a medium. He therefore could not agree with earlier philosophers, such as Galileo, who believed that light was a special sort of immaterial substance. Nor did he believe that anything had to travel from a light source to the eye for vision to occur. Instead, he gives the following account, mainly in the *Optical Treatise*, propositions 1–3, *Leviathan*, chapter 1 and *On Body*, chapter 25.

What makes a material object, such as the sun, a source of light is that it rapidly expands and contracts – Hobbes himself compared it to the diastole and systole (expansion and contraction) of the heart, and he may have been influenced by the way the stars appear to twinkle. Nothing is emitted from the light source, otherwise it would eventually disappear. Instead, space is filled with an extremely rarefied and tenuous ether which penetrates everything and is found everywhere. The pulsation of the light source sets up a similar pulsation in the parts of the ether next to it, and they in turn transmit it to the parts next to them, and so on until the motion is deflected by hitting a solid object, or absorbed into the eye. Since the pulsation is transmitted through an ever-increasing sphere of ether, its force becomes weaker, which explains why light sources appear dimmer and smaller the further away they are.

Although I have described the process as taking place over time, in fact Hobbes believed, along with most of his contemporaries, that the pulsation is transmitted instantaneously. He thought it was like pushing something with a stick, in which case (he believed) the far end of the stick moves at exactly the same time as you exert a force on the end in your hand. Hobbes simply did not consider the paradoxical implication of maintaining that causes and effects in a causal chain are simultaneous, namely that the whole history of the universe would be run through in an instant.

Hobbes insists that, so far, light has not yet come into existence, since there is nothing other than a vibrating physical medium. Light exists only when the vibrations are registered by a sentient observer. In his earlier writings, in particular the *Optical Treatise*, Hobbes gives the following account of how the sensation of light comes into being. On reaching the retina, the pulsation of the ether is transferred to the optic nerve, and carried down the nerve and into the brain. At this point it meets with an equal and opposite reaction, which sets up a similar motion back along the optic nerve and into the eye. It is this motion which Hobbes calls a 'phantasm' or 'fancy', from a Greek word meaning an appearance or sensory image.

Hobbes gives no explanation of how a motion in our physical body can be identical with what is immediately present to our minds when we perceive lights and colours. However, many philosophers would say that the problem of the relation between physical events in the body and conscious experience is intrinsically insoluble, and Hobbes was wise not to attempt the impossible. He is also unclear about where the phantasm is generated, but he seems to have held that it is at the outer surface of the eye, because he had a theory (which we shall look at later) that a phantasm is generated whenever two bodies interact, even if they are not sentient beings.

vi. SPECIAL FEATURES OF HOBBES'S ACCOUNT

Hobbes's account has a number of significant features which set him apart from most of his contemporaries. First, he is unashamedly materialist. Having stipulated that only matter in motion exists, he had to give an account of perception according to which our sensations are nothing other than motions in our material bodies. Although his explanatory apparatus is far too primitive to provide a plausible account of the whole perceptual process, he was quite adamant that any explanation would have to be in purely materialist terms. Interestingly, this was one point on which he and his arch-opponent Descartes were largely agreed. For Descartes, sensation was a purely materialist phenomenon, with sensory images being nothing other than motions of the 'animal spirits' in the cavities of the brain – and animal spirits consisted of rarefied matter which pervaded the human body, and accounted for its ability to perceive and act. However, Descartes had a problem Hobbes did not have, namely to explain how the immaterial soul could be conscious of material images in the brain. In fact, Descartes eventually gave up on the problem, and said that the union of the soul and the body was a mystery which we knew by experience to be the case, but which we could not rationally understand.

The second significant feature of Hobbes's theory is that he is the first to give a materialist explanation of why we perceive objects as being external to ourselves, and not merely as representations inside our heads. Others, such as Plato (in *Theaetetus* 156D–157B, and *Timaeus* 45A–46A) and certain scholastic philosophers, had maintained that we perceive objects by projecting onto them a 'visual stream' emanating from our eyes, rather like radar. But this visual stream is a complete fiction, and even if it existed, it would not explain how our brains register information about objects picked up by the visual stream. Hobbes, on the other hand, keeps the end-product of the perceptual process firmly within the human body, and has an ingenious, materialist explanation of why we perceive objects as external. It is because the phantasms which constitute our perceptions are motions, and the motions are directed outwards. Although the phantasms are internal to ourselves, their outward motion (or 'conation' as he sometimes calls it – we shall come to this term later) makes it seem to us that they are at a distance from our bodies, and not inside our heads.

The third significant feature is that Hobbes makes a distinction, in *On Body*, chapter 25 section 6, between having a phantasm and having a sensation. Although the article is titled 'One phantasm at a time', what he actually says is that we can have only one *sensation* at a time. Every object that affects our sensibility gives rise to a phantasm, but we can focus our attention only on one object at a time. As he says:

> It follows from this that not every outward conation of an organ is to be called a sensation, but only the one which is predominant and more forceful than the rest at any given time. It eliminates the phantasms of the other things just as the light of the sun eliminates the light of the other stars – not by impeding their action, but by obscuring and hiding them through its excess of brightness.

This is an early and unusually clear recognition of the role of the unconscious in human experience. At any given time, there are innumerable phantasms acting on us, but we are as unaware of them as we are unaware of the stars when the sun is shining. It is also an interesting anticipation of the philosophy of Kant, whose theory of knowledge was dominated by the principle that most of what goes on in our minds is below the threshold of consciousness, and that we can apprehend only one thing at a time.

vii. PERCEPTION AND ACTION

Earlier I said that this was Hobbes's earlier account. The one significant change he later made was to make the heart rather than the brain the endpoint of incoming sensations. Instead of rebounding directly from the brain to the sense organ, they went from the brain to the heart and then back again *via* the brain to the sense organ. The reason for this is that Hobbes, along with most of his contemporaries, believed that the heart was the seat of the emotions, and that the emotions were what stimulated us to action. Descartes had a complicated and wholly implausible theory about how incoming sensations might initiate bodily actions directly from the brain, with some modifications arising from the state of the heart, and direct intervention by the immaterial soul through the pineal gland. Hobbes did not have to explain interaction between physical sensations and the immaterial soul, because he did not believe in the latter. But he did need to explain the connection between incoming sensations and our bodily reactions to them.

Hobbes's theory was that the sensations must have some effect when they reach the heart, and this will either help or hinder its vital motion. In the former case we feel pleasure, and in the latter case we feel pain. Consequently the body pursues what gives it pleasure, and avoids what gives it pain. As he puts it in *On Body*, chapter 25 section 12:

> However, there is an entirely different kind of sensation, which I am going to say something about now. This is the sensation of *pleasure* or *pain*, which arises, not through an outward reaction of the heart, but through a continuous action from the outermost part of the organs towards the heart. Since the principle of life is in the heart, it is necessarily the case that a motion

propagated by the sentient being to the heart will change or divert the vital motion in some way or other – more specifically, by making it easier or more difficult, or by helping or impeding it. If it helps it, this gives rise to *pleasure*; if it impedes it, it gives rise to *pain, harm,* or *sickness.* And just as phantasms seem to exist outside us because of the outward conation, so when pleasure and pain are sensed, they seem to be within us, because of the inward conation of the organ. Indeed, they seem to be where the first cause of the pleasure or pain is – for example, if we are suffering pain from a wound, the pain seems to be where the wound itself is.

Hobbes's account is, of course, wrong. However, we must remember how little was known about the functioning of the human body at the time, and physicians were only in the earliest stages of treating the body as a physical object which obeyed the same laws of nature as everything else. In the very next paragraph of *On Body*, Hobbes mentions his friend William Harvey (1578–1657), who had discovered only a few decades earlier that the heart works like a mechanical pump. Hobbes's theory, however speculative, was an attempt to provide an equally mechanistic account of sensation and emotion.

viii. PRIMARY AND SECONDARY QUALITIES

Having looked at Hobbes's account of perception, we are now in a position to consider where he stood on the distinction between primary and secondary qualities. He does not actually use these terms himself, but his position can easily be deduced. Given his theory of perception, *all* the perceived qualities of things must be secondary qualities, and only in the mind. As he puts it in the *Elements of Law*, chapter 2 section 10:

> From this it also follows that, whatever accidents or qualities our senses make us think there are in the world, they are not out there, but are only seemings and appearances. The things which really exist in the world outside us are the motions by which these seemings are caused. And this is the great sensory illusion; but

one which is also to be corrected by sensation. For just as it is sensation which tells me, when I look directly at an object, that the colour seems to be in the object; so also it is sensation which tells me, when I look at a *reflected* object, that colour is *not* in the object.

Taken literally, what Hobbes says here is that only *motions* exist in the world outside us. This is a perfectly possible metaphysical position – for example, Plato in *Theaetetus*, 156A, says 'everything is motion, and nothing else exists.' But this is not Hobbes's actual position, because he believed that only *matter* could be in motion.

However, Hobbes is in something of a difficulty, if all that is given to us is secondary qualities. How can we know that there are primary qualities at all, and if so, what they are? In tackling this question, Hobbes has the imaginative idea of starting from the assumption that nothing exists, and then building up an account of external reality. In *On Body*, chapter 7 section 1, he writes:

> . . . the best way to begin an exposition of the philosophy of nature is to start from absence of being – that is, to imagine that the universe has ceased to exist. Let us suppose that everything has been annihilated, apart from yourself, who have escaped the holocaust. It might well be asked what is left for you to philosophise about, or to reason about at all, or what you could give a name to in order to reason about it.

> What I say is that you would retain the ideas of the world and of all the bodies which you had looked at with your eyes, or perceived with your other senses, before they were annihilated – in other words, a memory and imagination of sizes, motions, sounds, colours, etc., and also of their order and parts. Even if all these are only ideas or phantasms, and internal accidents of yourself who is imagining them, nevertheless they will appear to you as external, and independent of the powers of the mind. . . . But even if things have not been annihilated, if we pay careful attention to what we have in mind when we reason, the only things we make our calculations about are our phantasms. If we

make calculations about the sizes and motions of the heavens and the earth, it is not as if we literally travelled into the sky to divide the sky itself into its parts or measure its motions. Rather, we do it without moving anywhere, and in our studies, or with our eyes closed.

Here Hobbes seems to be making the strong claim that, if the external world were suddenly annihilated, we would not immediately notice, because we would still have phantasms which appear to us to be external. Moreover, since all we have is our phantasms, they are the only things we can reason about. We have no direct access to things as they are in themselves. We are still trapped in a subjective world of secondary qualities.

The next stage in Hobbes's argument is to bring in the concept of space, since obviously we cannot represent things as external to ourselves unless we have a subjective space in which extended objects are represented as distant from ourselves, as having spatial dimensions, and as being in spatial relations to each other.

In *On Body*, chapter 7 section 2, Hobbes says:

If we remember, or have a phantasm of something which existed before the supposed annihilation of external things; and if we have no interest in what sort of thing it was, but are only interested in the fact that it was external to the mind, then we have what is called *space*. It is certainly imaginary, since it is a mere phantasm; but it is precisely what everyone calls 'space'.

So space is still something subjective and imaginary, through which we represent things as being external to the mind. Hobbes has to say this, because, as a strict materialist, he cannot allow the objective existence of anything that is not a material object, and space is clearly not a material object. Many philosophers (for example Leibniz and Kant) have agreed with Hobbes that the idea of space as an objectively existing entity, which is not itself material but within which material objects exist, is incoherent, because it lacks the properties necessary for it to count as real. Empty space is just nothing, and nothingness cannot exist.

Then in *On Body*, chapter 8 section 1, Hobbes finally tells us what the primary qualities of matter are:

> We now understand the nature of imaginary space, in which we suppose nothing external to exist, but only the pure absence of the things which, when they existed, left their images in the mind. Let us next suppose that one of these things is put back again, or re-created. It is therefore necessary for that re-created or replaced thing not only to occupy some part of the said space (i.e. to coincide and be coextensive with it), but also to be something which does not depend on our imagination. But this is the very thing which is customarily called *body* on account of its extension; *self-subsistent* on account of its independence from our thought; *existent* because it subsists outside us; and finally *substance* or *subject* because it seems to support and underlie imaginary space, so that it is not by the senses, but only by reason that we understand that something is there. So the definition of body is something like this: *Body is whatever coincides or is coextensive with a part of space, and does not depend on our thought.*

Later in the chapter, Hobbes makes it clear that, in addition to extension, matter is characterized by the capacity to be in motion or at rest, and by solidity. This enables him, unlike Descartes, to make a conceptual distinction between solid material objects, and the rarefied ether surrounding them.

Two features of the above passage are worthy of comment. The first is that Hobbes insists that bodies are extended, but not *in* space. They cannot be *in* space, because Hobbes has said that space is only imaginary, and if bodies were in space, they too would be only imaginary. So, he has the subtle device of making bodies coextensive with space, without actually being in it. His idea is that we project images outwards, and these images are in imaginary space. Bodies themselves are, as it were, directly behind our images, and coextensive with them. Whether it makes sense to talk of bodies as being extended but without being in space is a moot point. Hobbes would no doubt say that there is no contradiction in simply asserting that body is extended, and that there is no way of deducing the existence of space from the extendedness of body, if by 'space' is meant an entity distinct from the body occupying it.

ix. SCIENTIFIC KNOWLEDGE

The other important feature in the above passage is that Hobbes says that we know of the existence of bodies, not by the senses, but by reason. This seems to put him in the same camp as Descartes, who held that our senses do not give us any information about reality as it is in itself, but only our reason can. Indeed, in *On Body*, chapter 6 sections 8 9, Hobbes gives exactly the same example as Descartes of our having two different ideas of the sun:

> . . . if you look at the sun, you will have a certain shining idea roughly a foot in diameter, and you will call it the sun, even if you know scientifically that the sun is really much larger.

However, there is one crucial difference between Hobbes and Descartes. For Descartes, the rational soul has its own source of knowledge of reality independently of the senses, namely innate ideas planted in the soul at birth by a non-deceiving God. For Hobbes, by contrast, human reason is wholly dependent on the senses for the content of its thoughts. In this he was following the orthodox dictum of scholastic Aristotelian philosophers that 'There is nothing in the understanding which was not previously in the senses.' So, we must now consider how Hobbes thought we could have knowledge of reality by reason, if there are no non-sensory ideas.

Hobbes distinguishes between two kinds of knowledge, using two different Latin words for them: *scientia* and *cognitio*. Unfortunately, the words 'science' and 'cognition' do not correspond to Hobbes's distinction, and I shall refer to them instead as 'scientific knowledge', and plain 'knowledge', or 'empirical knowledge'. In *On Body*, chapter 1 section 2, Hobbes states that empirical knowledge is something we share with other animals, since they too have senses (generally, unlike most of his contemporaries, Hobbes tends to emphasize the similarities rather than the differences between humans and animals). Examples of empirical knowledge are the knowledge we have when we perceive something, when we remember having perceived something or when we expect something to happen on the basis of past experience. Although he does not mention it here, elsewhere he includes knowledge derived from the testimony of others as empirical knowledge.

Scientific knowledge is knowledge we arrive at by reasoning, and it is exclusive to humans. He defines it as follows in *On Body*, chapter 6 section 1:

Philosophy is knowledge of phenomena or apparent effects acquired by right reasoning from a conception of some possible means of their production or coming into being; or knowledge of a means of production which actually occurred or could have occurred, from a conception of an apparent effect. Therefore the *method* of philosophising is *the most direct tracking down of effects through known causes, or of causes through known effects.* And we are said to have *scientific* knowledge of an effect *when we know both that its causes exist; and what subject the causes exist in; and what subject they bring about the effect in; and how they do it.* So scientific knowledge is knowledge 'why', or of causes; whereas all other knowledge is knowledge 'that', and consists in sensation, or memory, which is an imagination remaining after sensation.

So the first starting-points of our scientific knowledge of everything are the phantasms of sensation and imagination. We know by nature that these exist; but to know why they exist, or what causes they come from, requires reasoning . . . [R]easoning consists in composition and division (or resolution). Therefore any method for investigating the causes of things is either compositive, or resolutive, or partly compositive and partly resolutive. The resolutive method is usually called *analytic*, and the compositive *synthetic*.

This passage raises a number of issues. First, Hobbes embraces the 'resolutive-compositive' scientific method, which was distinctive of Galileo and his predecessors at Padua – though scholars disagree how far Hobbes was directly influenced by them. Resolution or analysis consists in breaking down a thing or a state of affairs into its component parts, and composition or synthesis consists in putting parts together to form a whole. In terms of cause and effect, resolution consists in finding the causes of known effects, and composition consists in finding the effects of known causes. A little later (in chapter 6 section 7), Hobbes adds that the analytic method consists in arguing from sensations to general principles, and the synthetic method consists in arguing from general principles to sensations. However, in chapter 25 section 1, he explains that, because there are different ways in which one and the same thing can be brought into being, only reasoning from known causes to effects, or synthesis, gives us certain knowledge. If we reason from known effects to causes, we can only know that the cause is a possible one, not that it is the exact way the effect was actually produced.

Second, although Hobbes talks in terms of causes and effects, his account is not limited to events in the material world. The term 'cause' had a wider use in his day, and he intended it to cover logic and mathematics as well. So in a logical deduction, the premises 'cause' the conclusion, and in geometry, geometrical figures are 'caused' by their method of construction, and a total in an arithmetical calculation is 'caused' by the numbers it is composed of. Since these are instances of composition or synthesis, logical and mathematical knowledge is absolutely certain.

Indeed, the apparent promise that we can have certainty in natural science by using the synthetic method turns out to be an illusion, since certainty is possible only in logic and mathematics, and a few other areas. The reason for this is that we have certain knowledge only of things we ourselves have created. In the case of manufactured objects, such as clocks, we know how they work, because we made them in a certain way. And even if we did not make them ourselves, we can take them apart (analyse them) and put them together again (synthesize them). The most significant example Hobbes gives of something we have made, and therefore can have perfect knowledge of, is the state. At the very beginning of the Introduction to *Leviathan*, he compares the state to an artificial animal created by humans, imitating the human body created by God. But since natural objects are created by God and not by us, and God has the power to create things in different possible ways, we cannot have certain, synthetic knowledge of how they were created. And the problem of knowing causes is made still worse by the fact that most of the causes of perceptible objects are themselves imperceptible (e.g. the motions of tiny corpuscles), so at best we can make plausible hypotheses about causes. The outcome, which may seem paradoxical to us, is that political philosophy is a proper science, like geometry, whereas physical science is merely guesswork. As Hobbes says in *On the Human Being* chapter 10 section 5:

> Most provable theorems are about quantity, the science of which is called 'geometry'. This is because the properties of individual shapes are inherent in the lines which we ourselves have drawn, and the generation of these figures depends on our will. Nothing more is required for knowing any transformation specific to that figure, other than that we take account of everything which follows from the act of construction we ourselves performed in drawing the figure. Therefore it happens that geometry is considered to be provable, and indeed is so, precisely because we ourselves create the figures.
>
> By contrast, we cannot deduce the properties of real things from their causes, because we do not see these causes – they are not in our power, but lie in the divine will; and the most significant of them, namely the ether, is invisible. However, by drawing consequences from the properties we do see, it is granted to us to advance as far as to be able to prove that such and such could have been their causes . . .
>
> Finally, politics and ethics, or the sciences of the just and the unjust, and of the right and the wrong, can be proved apriori. This is because we ourselves created the principles by which it is known what are the just and the right, and, conversely, the unjust and the wrong – that is, the causes of justice, namely laws and contracts. For until contracts and laws were established, there was no justice or injustice, nor was anything naturally for or against the public good among human beings, any more than among other animals.

Nevertheless, it is a powerful idea that, just as God has perfect knowledge of what he has created, we humans have perfect knowledge of the more restricted range of things we can create. It applies especially to geometry, where we know how to generate any possible geometrical figure. So, for example, we know with absolute certainty that the angles of a triangle are equal to two right-angles, because it follows from the way we create any triangle. This also has enormous implications for our knowledge of physical reality, because, although we are ignorant of specific causes, the essential property of matter is extension, and geometry is the science of extension. The size and shape of any material object can be described geometrically, and necessary conclusions can be derived from this description. Given the assumption that reality consists of extended matter in motion, it was not unreasonable to believe that geometry was half-way to providing a necessary science of nature. Though there was probably no direct influence, it is interesting that Kant, over a century later, gave the same justification for his theory that we can have necessarily true knowledge of how things will appear to us, because of what we contribute to the world as we perceive it.

x. LANGUAGE

What is still missing is an account of how human reason can move from receiving sensations to creating new knowledge about reality by the use of reason. Here Hobbes is at his most original, but also at his most vulnerable. First we must consider his account of language, which he gives in *On Body*, chapter 2, and more briefly in *Leviathan*, chapter 4.

All Hobbes's contemporaries believed that the possession of an immaterial, immortal, rational soul was what distinguished human beings from animals. Since Hobbes, uniquely, did not believe in the soul, he had to find another way of making the distinction. This was the ability to use language. Indeed, he played with the traditional definition of man as a rational animal, by pointing out that the primary meaning of the Greek word for 'rational' (*logikos*) was 'capable of speech'. The consequence of this was that Hobbes laid far greater stress on the importance of language for philosophy than any other philosopher until the 'linguistic turn' of the twentieth century.

For Hobbes, words (or 'names' as he usually calls them) have two functions. Their first function is as 'notes', by which we record our thoughts, or mental images. Although it is possible to have thought processes that consist solely of a sequence of images, Hobbes claims that we would easily forget what conclusions we had come to, and would have no means of recalling them. By giving names to our images, we create a sort of mental filing system, which enables us to retrieve past thoughts at will. The second function of names is as 'signs'. As long as language consists only of notes, it remains private to an individual, and no-one can tell anyone else the outcome of their thinking. So communities have to agree which names refer to which images, so that individuals can communicate with each other.

These are by no means the only advantages of language. Without language:

- Our brains would be overwhelmed with a mass of information about individual experiences. Everything in nature is individual, and there are no 'universals', or abstract entities corresponding to classes of things, as philosophers such as Plato believed. Nor do we have abstract concepts in our minds, which might have the same function. But names can refer to aspects of things that are common to many individuals, thus enabling us to have thoughts applying to indefinitely many individuals without our having to think through each one.
- We would be restricted to contingent facts about individual things or events. But scientific knowledge requires universal and necessary laws. It is only through names with universal application that scientific knowledge becomes possible.
- Arithmetic is impossible without a system of notation. Someone without language can hear a clock strike – bong, bong, bong – but only by having memorized the names 'one', 'two', 'three', etc., can that person know how many times it has struck.
- The fact that humans have language is a fact; but it cannot be registered simply through perceptual images. In order for us

to discuss the nature of language, we need what Hobbes calls 'names of the second intention', or what we might call 'meta-names' or names of names. These are possible only if we have a language.

So far, so good. But there are problems with Hobbes's account of language. The first problem is that he says that our choice of names is *arbitrary*. That is to say, we are completely free what to call what. Now, in one sense it is true to say that names have no intrinsic relation to what they name, apart from a small number of onomato-poeic names which resemble what they denote, such as 'cuckoo', or a dog's 'bark'. This is obvious from the fact that the same things have utterly different names in different languages. But the problem is that, if we are to have a shared understanding of what words mean, we cannot simply label images in our minds, because they are not accessible to others. We need to provide definitions.

Hobbes was all too aware of this. In *On Body*, chapter 6 sections 13–15, he gives his theory of definition. He lays such stress on definitions that he attacks the traditional geometrical method, according to which theorems are demonstrated as following from definitions and self-evident axioms. According to Hobbes, axioms are unnecessary, because the theorems will follow directly from well constructed definitions. And indeed he practises what he preaches. Apart from one brief experiment with the traditional geometrical method (the *Optical Treatise*), Hobbes's writings are characterized by an abundance of definitions matched by few other philosophers.

But if definitions are entirely arbitrary, it is difficult to see how truth can follow from them. In the game of chess, we can define with absolute precision the rules of the game and the moves each piece can make, but this does not tell us anything about reality. Similarly, the definitions of Euclidean geometry prescribe a closed system, which may or may not correspond to reality – and the lesson of modern science is that it does not exactly.

So, if scientific knowledge is to be deducible from definitions of names, these definitions cannot be entirely arbitrary. Hobbes implicitly recognizes this when he says that some definitions are better than others, and lays down criteria for what constitutes a good definition. The most important feature of a good definition is that it includes the cause of the thing defined. As he says in *On Body*, chapter 6 section 13:

> The reason why I say that those [things] which have a cause and a way of coming into being should be defined in terms of their cause and way of coming into being, is as follows. The purpose of demonstration is scientific knowledge of the causes of things, and of how they come into being. But if it does not feature in the definitions, it cannot feature in the conclusion of the first syllogism derived from the definitions. And if it does not feature in the first conclusion, it cannot feature in any subsequent conclusion. Therefore there cannot ever be any scientific knowledge of it, which is inconsistent with the purpose and intention of the demonstrator.

It is clear from an example he gives earlier in this article that he is thinking primarily of geometry here:

> But in the case of names of things which can be understood as having a cause, that cause or way of being generated must itself be included in the definition – for example, when we define a circle as a shape created by rotating a straight line on a plane.

A significant proportion of Euclid's *Elements* consists in methods for constructing particular figures, rather than proofs of propositions. The equipment you are allowed for constructing them (whether drawing them in sand or on paper, or just in your imagination) is a scribe for drawing with, an unmarked straight edge, and a pair of compasses. Hobbes's central idea was that the most basic figures should be defined, not through a static description of their properties, but through the way they are constructed using this equipment. Thus, Hobbes's example of the definition of a circle implies the use of a pair of compasses, which preserves the same straight line between its points. It is quite different from Euclid's own definition of a circle, which is:

A *circle* is a plane figure contained by one line such that all the straight lines falling upon it from one point among those lying within the figure equal one another.

As we saw earlier, we can have demonstrative knowledge in geometry, because geometrical figures are things we ourselves create, rather than just finding them in nature, created for us by God. By contrast, our knowledge of physical objects is only hypothetical, because we cannot know how God actually created things. We saw in *On Body*, chapter 6 section 1, how Hobbes said that we know by reason what the causes of our sensations are. But when we come to his actual explanation in chapter 25 section 1, he has to back-track because of our lack of knowledge:

Consequently, there are two methods of philosophizing. One is from the way something comes into being to its possible effects, and the other is from effects revealed in experience to a way they possibly came into being. In the first of these, it is we ourselves who are responsible for the truth of the primary principles of reasoning (namely definitions), by agreeing on the names of things. I have carried out this first part in the preceding chapters; and, unless I am mistaken, I have asserted nothing other than definitions and what follows from them. That is to say, I have asserted nothing which I have not sufficiently demonstrated to those who agree with me as to the usage of words – and these are the only people I have business with.

I now embark on the second part, which proceeds from the phenomena or effects of nature known to us by sensation, to the investigation of some way in which, I do not say they *did* come into being, but in which they *could* have come into being. Consequently, the starting points which are the basis of what follows are not created by ourselves, nor are they asserted universally, as definitions are. Rather, we observe what has been placed in things themselves by the author of nature, and we employ singular rather than universal propositions. Again, they do not amount to the necessity characteristic of a theorem, but only show the *possibility* of some particular way of coming into being – though not without the universal propositions already demonstrated above.

So, if we return to the question of how we know that matter exists and what its primary qualities are, the answer has to be that we cannot know with the certainty of a geometrical proposition. But by using our reason, we can make the plausible hypothesis that we have sensations because objects act upon our sense organs, and that the primary qualities of these objects are the minimum necessary to give plausible explanations of all natural phenomena.

xi. REASONING

As for what reasoning consists in, Hobbes departs radically from any idea of its being a mysterious, almost magical power given to us by God. Instead he reduces it to the simplest of operations. The very title of Part I of *On Body* says it all: 'Computation, or Logic'. He assumes that the basic arithmetical operations of adding and subtracting are unproblematic. We can count because we have an arbitrary set of names in a fixed order, such that each number is one larger than its predecessor. We count physical objects by naming the first one 'one', the second one 'two', the third one 'three' and so on until there are no objects left to count. We can add another group of objects by continuing from where we left off, and we can subtract by counting backwards. Hobbes's originality consists in his idea that adding and subtracting (computation) are the archetype of all reasoning, thus depriving it of any mystery.

As we have seen, what we have in our minds when reasoning is names functioning as notes (though Hobbes does allow a primitive form of non-verbal reasoning). These names can be added or subtracted, so as to form more or less general names. For example, if you add 'rational' to 'animal', you get 'rational animal', which is the definition of a human being. Since humans are a sub-set of animals, adding the name 'rational' makes the name more specific. Conversely, by subtracting 'rational' from 'rational animal', you get 'animal', which is more general than 'human being'.

Similarly, we can add names to form propositions, linking them with the verb 'to be' (at least in languages like Latin or English); and propositions themselves can be added and subtracted. As Hobbes puts it in *Leviathan* chapter 5 (CL 22):

> Logicians too do the same with sequences of words, adding two names together to make a proposition, and two propositions together to make a syllogism, and a number of syllogisms to make a proof; and from the sum or conclusion of a syllogism they subtract one proposition to find another.

xii. AN ALTERNATIVE THEORY OF MEANING

Earlier, we looked at Hobbes's theory of meaning, according to which the primary function of names is as notes for recording our private thoughts, and their use as signs to communicate our thoughts to others is secondary. He also stresses their arbitrary nature, which suggests that any use of language is legitimate and meaningful, provided only that it is internally consistent. Indeed, it may well be that Lewis Carroll had Hobbes specifically in mind when he wrote the following in *Through the Looking Glass* (*p. 196*):

> 'When *I* use a word', Humpty Dumpty said, in a rather scornful tone, 'it means just what I choose it to mean – neither more nor less.'

> 'The question is', said Alice, 'whether you *can* make words mean so many different things.'

> 'The question is', said Humpty Dumpty, 'which is to be the master – that's all.'

Like Humpty Dumpty, Hobbes seems to be giving anyone the power to invent words and to use them how they like. However, as we have already seen in *Leviathan* chapter 1 (CL 7), Hobbes is scathing about meaningless language in universities:

But because I am later going to talk about their function in society, I must let you see what things need to be corrected in them whenever the occasion arises. The frequency of meaningless language is one.

Failure to give definitions at all, or giving logically inconsistent definitions, may account for some meaningless language. And Hobbes does indeed provide some analyses of contradictions in the language of university philosophy. But his attack on what he considers to be meaningless language goes much wider than this. He wants to dismiss virtually all the philosophy and science taught at university as not merely wrong, but meaningless; and likewise most theology, especially Catholic theology. His official theory of meaning gives him almost no scope for accusing others of meaninglessness. But in a few passages, he introduces an entirely different theory which does do the trick. Interestingly, the change in theory almost exactly anticipates a change in theory undergone by Ludwig Wittgenstein (1889–1951), who in his early work the *Tractatus* took an individualist approach like Hobbes's, but in his later *Philosophical Investigations* argued against the very possibility of a private language, and maintained that language is primarily a social phenomenon. Hobbes's new criterion for meaningfulness is that anything must be translatable into any 'copious' vernacular language as used by ordinary people. As he says in the English version of *Leviathan* chapter 8 (CL 46):

There is yet another fault in the language of some people, which may also be included as a kind of madness, namely the abuse of words called absurdity, which I spoke about in chapter 5. This is when people utter words which have no meaning at all in the way they are put together . . . This affects only those, like university teachers, who discuss incomprehensible things, or in questions of abstruse philosophy. Ordinary people hardly ever talk meaninglessly, and they are therefore branded as idiots by the intellectual élite. But we need some examples to show that their words have nothing corresponding to them in their minds. Take into your hands a book written by an academic, and see if you can translate any chapter on any difficult point (such as the Trinity, God, the nature of Christ, transubstantiation, free will, etc.) into any modern language so as to make it intelligible, or into any acceptable Latin as was known to those for whom it was their ordinary language. What is the meaning of these words? – 'The first cause does not necessarily inflow any thing into the second, by force of the essential subordination of the second causes, by which it may help it to work.' This is the translation of the title of the sixth chapter of the first book of Suárez's *Of the Concourse, Motion, and Help of God*. When people write whole volumes of such stuff, are they not mad, or intending to make others mad?

And again in chapter 46 (CL 467):

I could produce more examples of vacuous philosophy introduced into religion by university teachers of theology; but other people can observe them for themselves if they wish. I shall add only this, that the writings of theology teachers are mostly nothing other than meaningless strings of strange and barbarous words, or words used in senses other than the everyday use of the Latin language, such as would be practised by Cicero, Varro, and all the grammarians of ancient Rome. If anyone wants proof of this, let them (as I have said once before) see whether they can translate any writings of a theology teacher into any modern language, such as French, English, or any other copious language. For that which cannot be made intelligible in most of these languages is not intelligible in Latin.

This is wonderful rhetoric. But just as Hobbes's official theory of language is too liberal in tolerating possible nonsense, his alternative theory is too restrictive in outlawing any technical terminology. The weasel word is 'copious'. What is to count as a 'copious' language? Clearly not the Latin of university teachers, which is *too* copious. And presumably not languages such as Gaelic or German, in which no one had yet thought of writing philosophy. He gives French and English as examples, but again he can hardly be thinking of the limited vocabularies of the peasantry. He must be thinking of the French and English of the intellectual circles he moved in. But if so, his reasoning is circular. He and his fellow modern philosophers had developed a vocabulary in which they could express their mechanistic world view, and they rejected the world view they were overthrowing as meaningless, because it contained innumerable items which could not be translated into their own relatively simplistic terminology. This is not to say that the modern philosophers were wrong, but that Hobbes's linguistic argument is insufficient. Modern science is radically untranslatable into ordinary language, but that does not mean that it is meaningless.

CHAPTER 3

MATERIALISM

i. INTRODUCTION

The medieval world was full of all sorts of beings other than matter in motion. For example, there were space and time (as distinct from the bodies and events they contained), universals (or abstract forms common to members of the same species), essences, underlying substances, numbers, perfect geometrical figures, truths, moral values, final causes, sensible species, occult powers and virtues, immaterial souls, angels, spirits, ghosts and an immaterial God. Hobbes denied the existence of all of these, and he held that every phenomenon of nature and human experience could be explained as nothing other than the product of matter in motion.

We have already seen how Hobbes rejected some of these things. He argued that space was merely a subjective phantasm, and that bodies could be extended without being *in* an imperceptible, immaterial and totally mysterious real space. He argued that all we needed for arithmetic was numbers, and that numbers were nothing other than arbitrary signs which we recite in a fixed order. And he argued that the theory of sensible species completely failed to explain how we perceive things, unlike his own theory that we perceive when external objects exert a pressure on our sense organs. The purpose of the present chapter is to look at the most important of the other ways in which Hobbes reduced phenomena to matter in motion, though we shall leave discussion of God to Chapter 6.

ii. SUBSTANCE

Medieval philosophy spawned a wide range of theories of substance, which are sometimes difficult to disentangle from each other. The concept of substance was brought in to fulfil a number of functions, including the following:

- There is a crucial distinction between merely having sensory images, and having sensory images of an object which actually exists. One way of making the contrast is to say that in the latter case the images are of qualities which inhere in an underlying substance (and the Latin *substantia* literally means that which 'stands under' perceived qualities). The substance and its qualities continue to exist when not being perceived, whereas mere images exist only as long as they are being perceived.

- Qualities and relations cannot exist by themselves, but must be qualities *of* things, or relations *between* things. They are like waves, which can exist only in a medium which is subject to wave motion (drain the water from a lake, and there will be no more waves in it). So there must be substances, which are distinct from perceived qualities or relations, and in which the latter inhere.

- Things change. But for it to make sense to say that one and the same thing has changed, rather than having been replaced by something else, there must be something which remains the same before and after the change. This is the substance underlying the perceived qualities. If my grandfather had an axe, and changed the handle, and then bequeathed it to my father, who changed the blade, it would not be the same axe, because there was no substance in common between the original axe, and the one I inherited from my father.

The position is complicated by the fact that, in addition to the generic concept of an underlying substance, many philosophers used the term to mean an individual entity capable of independent existence. In this sense, Socrates would be an individual substance, consisting of his generic underlying substance together with all his individuating qualities; whereas his wisdom would not be a substance, since it could exist only as the quality of an individual substance.

There are many problems with the concept of substance, of which the most serious is that it is by definition unobservable. As we have seen, Hobbes held that the only source of ideas in our minds is sense impressions or phantasms, of which our thoughts are faded after-images. Consequently we can have no idea at all of things we cannot perceive, such as substance. All our senses present us with are material objects or bodies, and we can have no conception of substance as something different from and additional to body. Therefore, we cannot have any conception of a substance which could support the properties of material objects, let alone those of any other kind of being.

iii. IMMATERIAL SUBSTANCES

However, there is a complication, namely that it does not follow logically from the fact that something is incomprehensible to human beings that it does not exist. Indeed, in his earlier writings, Hobbes clearly believes that angels exist, and that they are immaterial, and that their nature is totally incomprehensible to us. In the fifth objection to Descartes' *Meditations*, he writes:

> But when people think of angels, they sometimes have in their minds an image of a flame, and sometimes an image of a pretty little boy with wings. This makes me feel certain that the image does not resemble an angel, and therefore that it is not an idea of an angel. But since I believe that there do exist various created beings which serve God, and that they are invisible and immaterial, I apply the name 'angel' to the thing I believe in or suppose to exist, even though the idea through which I imagine an angel is a compound of ideas of visible things.

Presumably at this time he believed that it was an article of faith that there were immaterial beings, and that his religion gave him sufficient grounds for believing that they existed, even though they were incomprehensible. Later, however, he came to the view that, since there is no mention of immaterial substances anywhere in the Bible, he was not required to believe in their existence. So, given that he had no reason to believe in them, it was rational for him to believe that they did not exist. Consequently, the scope of the word 'substance' was co-extensive with the word 'body', and they could be used interchangeably. Thus, he writes in *Leviathan* chapter 34 (CL 262):

> According to this interpretation of the word 'body', 'body' and 'substance' have the same meaning; and consequently the compound expression 'incorporeal substance' is as meaningless as if you were to say 'non-bodily body.' And neither that expression, nor the word 'immaterial' is to be found anywhere in Holy Scripture.

And the very title of his work *On Body* is a powerful statement of his identification of body and substance, since a more traditional author writing on the same topics would have titled it *On Substance*.

As for angels, Hobbes was uncertain whether they were spirits in the sense of highly rarefied matter, or whether they were no more than visions conjured up by God when he wanted to communicate with mortals. For example, in *Leviathan* chapter 34 (CL 267), he writes:

> If we consider the passages in the Old Testament where angels are mentioned, we will find that (usually if not always) the word 'angel' denotes some sort of an idea which God conjures up in the phantasy, in order to signify the divine presence in some supernatural action of his.

By contrast, he has no doubt that belief in ghosts is pure superstition. In *Leviathan* chapter 2 (CL 10), after discussing the difficulty of distinguishing a vivid dream from reality, he writes:

> Even people who are wide awake are liable to the same kind of imaginations, if they are timid, superstitious, obsessed with reading horror stories, or alone in the dark. They believe that they see

ghosts and the spirits of the dead walking around in graveyards, whereas in fact they see nothing other than mere phantasms. Alternatively, they might have been duped by tricksters, who take advantage of their superstitious fears by disguising themselves in the clothes of the dead, and cross graveyards and other con-secrated ground during the night, so as to get to places it would be thought shameful for them to frequent too often.

He then goes on to discuss witchcraft. He denies that witches have any real power, but he holds that they deserve punishment because they believe that they have evil powers, and do their best to exercise them. Nowadays, Hobbes's rejection of superstitious beliefs seems quite unremarkable, but it is largely thanks to him that this is so. He was writing at the time when the craze for witch-hunting was at its height, and denial of the existence of immaterial substances was seen as atheistic. Despite his claim that he had a cowardly disposition, it took tremendous courage to espouse enlightened views before the Age of Enlightenment had begun.

iv. THE HUMAN SOUL

In Hobbes's day, the standard theory of the nature of the human soul was the Aristotelian one that it is the form of the body. Aristotle held that everything is a compound of form and matter. The form or essence consists of one or more general characteristics by virtue of which an individual substance belongs to a particular kind or species, whereas the matter consists of all its remaining character-istics, by virtue of which it is a unique individual. For Aristotle, the defining characteristic which distinguishes humans from everything else is their possession of reason ('Man is a rational animal'). Con-sequently, reason is the form of humans, as contrasted with all their bodily characteristics which make up their matter. It was only a short step to identify this reason or intellect with the soul.

Opinion is divided as to whether or not Aristotle believed that the soul could exist independently, and thus achieve immortality. Certainly the most logical conclusion is that it cannot, because, if it is nothing other than the form of the body, it will cease to exist when the body is destroyed. No one believes that the form of a table or of a cabbage or of a cat continues to exist after they have been destroyed, so why should humans be the single exception? This was a serious problem for St Thomas Aquinas (1225–1274), when he effectively made Aristotelianism the official philosophy of Catholic Christianity, since belief in personal immortality is central to Christianity. His solution was to appeal to the concept of *spirit*, as a type of substance which was half-way between the material and the completely immaterial – like a ghost (and in some languages, such as German, there is a single word meaning both 'spirit' and 'ghost'). Since the soul needed a body to exist in, God would supply it with a spiritual body.

One of the ways in which Descartes' philosophy was revolutionary was his belief that the soul was a substance in its own right. Apart from God himself, there were two kinds of substance, each with their exclusive defining property. There was matter, of which the essence was extension (the geometrical properties of size and shape), and mind or soul, the essence of which was thought. All the individual properties of these substances were 'modes' or particular manifestations of their essences. A material particle would have a particular shape and size, but none of the non-geometrical properties, such as colours and sounds, which exist only in the mind of the perceiver. A mind will always be thinking in one way or another; but it cannot have any of the properties which belong only to matter, namely shape and size.

Given that mind and body have absolutely nothing in common, Descartes had a serious problem explaining how they could affect each other, or even how a non-spatial mind could be intelligibly said to be 'in' a particular body. On the other hand, it did give him a much more convincing argument for the immortality of the soul than could be marshalled by the Aristotelian theologians of Catholicism. Since the mind and the body were entirely distinct entities, there was no reason why the mind should not continue to exist after the destruction of the body. It would still depend on the divine will to be kept in existence, but God did not need to miraculously create a mysterious spiritual body for this to be possible.

Descartes' theory of the mind was far from entirely original – it was very much in the tradition of Plato and St Augustine (364–430). However, it is an indication of Descartes' long-term influence that the Aristotelian theory has faded into insignificance, and in modern debates about the mind/body problem, the only serious contenders are Cartesian dualism, and Hobbesian materialism, to which we now turn.

We have already seen how Hobbes moved to his mature position that, since we can have no conception of immaterial substance, there is no conceptual distinction between substance and body, and the expression 'immaterial substance' is a contradiction in terms. It directly follows that the human mind cannot be an immaterial substance independent of the body.

However, just as Descartes had *his* problems over how there can be any interaction between mind and body, Hobbes too had his own problems. It is an obvious fact that we are conscious of ourselves and of our environment, and that we can change the material world by applying our intelligence and will to it. But it is difficult to explain how we can do these things if we are ultimately no more than material objects, like sticks or stones. Hobbes's great achievement was to think up some practical ideas for explaining how all human behaviour can be reduced to motions of a material body.

Hobbes and Descartes agreed that animals were purely material automata. They both rejected the ancient and scholastic idea that animals had 'animal souls' as a principle of life. Instead, they held that animals were alive as long as they were capable of moving themselves. Descartes went a long way towards explaining human activity as nothing other than mechanical functions. In his unpublished *Treatise on the Human Being*, he outlined a theory according to which sensations consisted of patterns of 'animal spirits', or rarefied matter like the vapour evaporating from brandy, which bounced off the pineal gland in the cavity in the centre of the brain, and were deflected down nerves leading to the muscles, and pumped up the muscles to make the limbs move. Which nerves they entered depended on the position of the pineal gland, which was moved by other animal spirits rising from the heart as the seat of the emotions. So, on seeing a lion, a person in a state of fear would run away from it, and one in a state of courage would approach it. In short, a human body without a soul would in many respects behave in exactly the same way as one with a soul – it would just be on automatic pilot, as it were.

Where Hobbes and Descartes differ is that Hobbes reduced *all* human activity to bodily motions, whereas Descartes held that there are at least two functions which could be explained only as due to the presence of an immaterial soul. These were thought and speech involving abstract concepts, and moral acts of the will directing the body to behave otherwise than it would naturally have done.

Descartes' actual argument for the existence of an immaterial soul is his famous *cogito* argument: 'I think therefore I exist'. His point is that he could imagine away the whole of the material world, including his own body, as non-existent; but he could not imagine away the thought that nothing else existed. But there cannot be a thought without a thinker, therefore he must exist as a thinking being or soul. And since he can conceive of his being able to think without anything material existing, his thinking soul must be immaterial and independent of the body.

In the second objection to the *Meditations*, Hobbes makes two criticisms of the argument. The first criticism is that, although Descartes is correct that there cannot be a thought without a thinker, he has not established that the thinker must be immaterial. In all our experience, it is material objects that are subject to actions, and we cannot conceive of any alternative. There is no reason to suppose that human thought is an exception: human beings are bodies that are distinguished from other bodies by the capacity to think:

> . . . it could be that a thinking thing is that which underlies mind, reason, or understanding as its subject, and hence that it is something corporeal. Mr. Descartes assumes without proof that it is not corporeal. And yet the conclusion he seems to want to establish depends on this inference . . . It seems to follow that a thinking thing is something corporeal. This is because it seems that the subjects of all actions are comprehensible only if they are conceived as corporeal or material.

The second criticism is, in effect, the criticism later made by Hume and Kant that the subject of thought cannot simultaneously be its own object, otherwise there is an infinite regress:

> Even though you can think about your having thought (this form of thinking is nothing other than remembering), it is absolutely impossible for you to think about your present thinking, any more than you can know that you know. That would lead to an infinite regress: how do you know that you know that you know that you know?

This may seem a rather abstract and dogmatic objection, but it can be illustrated by a physical analogy. If you look into a mirror, the pupil of your eye is black – you cannot see the retina by means of which you see everything else. Even if you are in an optometrist's chair, with a mirror in front of you and the optometrist examining your retina with a torch, you can only see the light of the torch and not your retina. This is not just a physical issue, but a logical one: if we are to have knowledge at all, there must be an ultimate subject (whether it is the retina or thought), which cannot be an object to itself.

So far I have studiously avoided using the term 'consciousness', because neither Descartes nor Hobbes used it in the modern sense of the special sort of self-awareness which is peculiar to humans (though recently some have argued that the higher primates might have something analogous to human consciousness). Both of them talk about 'thinking', which means reasoning with abstract concepts, but neither of them articulated a distinctive concept of peculiarly human consciousness. This conceptual innovation was due to Locke (1632–1704), and independently Leibniz (1646–1716), using the term *apperception* to mean the same thing.

Nevertheless, both Hobbes and Descartes clearly held that there was a difference in kind between humans and animals, in that humans have a capacity for self-awareness that is lacking in animals. Descartes' *cogito* argument makes no sense if the soul is not aware of itself. Hobbes is more elusive, because he wants to stress the continuities between humans and other animals, and when he discusses their differences it is more to do with their intellectual powers than with their capacity for introspection. However, we have already seen that, for Hobbes, the defining characteristic of a rational animal is the ability to use words, and he applies this to the question of consciousness in the sixth objection to Descartes' *Meditations*. Here, he makes it clear that animals might have the same thoughts as humans, where by 'thoughts' he means a sequence of mental images, but only humans can accompany the thoughts with a linguistic judgment about truth or falsehood, as a sort of running commentary on their experiences:

> Besides, assertion and negation cannot exist without language and names, which is why animals cannot assert or deny anything; nor can they exist without thought, which is why dumb animals cannot make judgments either. All the same, thought can be similar in humans and animals. When we assert that a person is running, we do not have a thought which is any different from that had by a dog watching its owner running. So the only thing that assertion or negation adds to simple thoughts is perhaps the thought that the names which the assertion consists of are the names of the same things in the mind of the person doing the asserting. This is not to involve in a thought anything more than its resemblance to its object, but to involve that resemblance twice over.

'To involve that resemblance twice over' is a nice way of giving expression to the fact that we don't simply know things, but that we know that we know them. And everything stops just there, otherwise we would enter the infinite regress mentioned above of knowing that we know that we know.

v. NO VACUUM

Hobbes seems to have assumed that it followed from his identification of substance with matter that there could be no empty space. Thus, in the English *Leviathan*, chapter 46 (CL 459), he writes:

The world (by which I mean not just the earth, ... but the *universe*, that is, the whole mass of all things that exist) is corporeal (that is to say, body) and has the dimensions of magnitude (namely, length, breadth, and depth). Also, every part of body is also body, and has the same dimensions. And consequently, every part of the universe is body, and that which is not body is no part of the universe. And because the universe is everything, that which is no part of it is nothing (and consequently, nowhere).

The last sentence excludes the possibility of a vacuum, because, if someone claims that a vacuum exists, it must exist *somewhere* (in a vacuum flask, for instance). But, Hobbes's argument makes sense only if he is treating a vacuum as some sort of an immaterial entity, like a human soul or an angel. For it does indeed follow from the proposition that everything which exists is material, that there are no immaterial entities. But if you consider a vacuum not to be an entity at all, but merely the absence of being, then Hobbes's argument is invalid. There is no contradiction in saying that everything which exists is material, but there are some places where nothing at all exists. If you can pump all the matter out of a vessel, then there is a vacuum, the position of which is determined by the walls of the vessel.

In his earlier writings, Hobbes did believe that there were small quantities of empty space, but he seems to have changed his mind in 1648. In a postscript to a letter to Mersenne of 17 February 1648, in which he had discussed Torricelli's experiments with a mercury thermometer, he writes:

It is said that when the mercury descends down the [glass] tube, it leaves behind a place containing a vacuum. But it is possible to see through that place, from which it follows that the action of a luminous body is propagated through a vacuum – which seems to me to be impossible. I would like you to find out, if you can, what shape is possessed by the perceived images of the things observed through that vacuum, in case the rays are transmitted, not through the vacuum itself, but in a circular motion through the body of the tube which contains the vacuum.

The idea that light rays might travel with a circular motion through the glass of the tube instead of in straight lines is highly imaginative. While it is hardly an anticipation of the modern concept of curved space-time or the invention of fibre-optic cable, it certainly shows Hobbes as commendably open-minded. However, nothing more is heard of this idea, and Hobbes rapidly came to the conclusion that there cannot be a vacuum, precisely because light is propagated in a straight line through places from which all air appears to have been removed.

The argument, which is far better than the previous one, is that light can only be propagated through a physical medium. As we have seen, Hobbes's theory was that light is propagated by each part of the ether pushing against the next part. If there is no ether, light cannot be transmitted. So, if we imagine all the matter being pumped out of a glass jar, it will become darker and darker, until ultimately no light can be transmitted through it at all. This is not the place to go into the nineteenth- and the twentieth-century arguments about the existence of the ether, but in the context of Hobbes's time, it was perfectly reasonable to claim that, if we can see through an apparent vacuum, there must either be a material medium supporting a wave motion through it, or there must be material light particles (photons) passing through it. Either way, it is not really a vacuum, and any alternative theory will have to appeal to immaterial and superstitious forces. According to Hobbes, the atmosphere consists of a mixture of denser air, which might conceivably be pumped out of perfectly sealed bodies, and more rarefied ether, which can pass between the particles constituting their walls. The ether is everywhere, and it cannot be pumped out of anything.

Hobbes addresses the question of the vacuum in *On Body*, chapter 6, but what he says is surprisingly uninformative, given arguments such as the above which he has at his disposal. Here he rests his positive case on a single phenomenon which he argues can be explained only on the assumption that there is no vacuum (a kind of watering jar which can be turned off by blocking the air intake). The bulk of his case is negative, criticizing the arguments in favour of a vacuum in *On the Nature of Things* by the Ancient Roman philosopher Lucretius (c. 99–55 BC).

Some years later, the scientist Robert Boyle (1627–1691) claimed to have succeeded in building a vacuum pump and creating an actual vacuum. Hobbes attacked the claim in a book called *A Dialogue about Physics* (1661), and Boyle responded in his (inaccurately titled) *Animadversions upon Mr. Hobbes's Problemata de Vacuo* (1674). In his attack, Hobbes makes the mistake of trying to deny that Boyle had actually succeeded in removing the air from a glass vessel (at least partly), and of giving wholly implausible alternative explanations of observed phenomena, such as the death of small animals in the vessel. In his turn, Boyle failed to understand Hobbes's reasons for believing in an all-pervasive ether. In fact, the two philosophers passed each other in the night. Boyle (along with his fellow members of the Royal Society) would accept only the evidence of the senses as confirmed by a group of observers, and regarded anything else as mere metaphysical hypotheses with no scientific basis. Hobbes, on the other hand, held that the outcomes of sensory experience were merely 'natural history', whereas genuine science had to consist in necessary and universal truths derived from real definitions. For Boyle, the vacuum was an experimental fact; for Hobbes, the existence of the ether was a necessary condition for the propagation of light.

vi. UNIVERSALS

One of the classic controversies of medieval philosophy was over the question of universals. A universal is that which embraces a whole class of things, as contrasted with a word or concept which refers to a particular individual. For example, the concept of 'The Earth', or the name 'Thomas Hobbes' are particulars, denoting just one thing each; whereas 'cat', or 'good' embrace all actual or possible cats or good things. In the case of particulars, there is no problem over what the terms refer to: 'The Earth' refers straightforwardly to the planet we inhabit, and the name 'Thomas Hobbes' refers to the famous philosopher from Malmesbury. In the case of universals, while everyone would agree that the words apply to more than one individual, there are three different theories about how they do so.

The first theory is *realism*. According to realists, different species of things are really different in nature. It is an objective fact that cats are different from dogs, and that gold is different from silver. This must be because the members of each species have something in common with each other, which they do not share with the members of other species. When we make assertions about the nature of a species as a whole, we are referring only to this common element, and not to the individual members with their different individuating characteristics. So if I say 'The human being is a rational animal', I am referring to humanity in general, and not to Peter who is short, balding, and fat, or to Jane who is slim, blonde and rides a motorbike. As for what the common element is, there are two classic theories.

The first version of realism is that of Plato ('universals before things'), according to which there are 'forms' or 'ideas', outside the world of space and time, which constitute the essence of each species. Individual things are imperfect copies of the form of the species to which they belong, and fall short of the ideal because of their varied individuating characteristics. We can recognize individuals as more or less closely resembling the ideal, but nothing on Earth can match the perfection of the ideal. For example, there is an ideal circle which has exactly the geometrical properties by which it is defined, but an earthly circle drawn in the sand, or any circular object made with a lathe or a potter's wheel will not have exactly those properties. As for how we can know the forms, Plato had an implausible metaphysical theory that our immaterial souls exist before as well as after life on earth, and in their previous existence they know the forms through direct acquaintance, since both souls and forms are immaterial, and like is known by like. On being joined to a human body, our souls forget the forms, but are gradually reminded of them because of their similarity to the objects of everyday experience.

The second version of realism is that of Aristotle ('universals in things'). Aristotle rejected the metaphysics of his teacher Plato, and held instead that, while forms are indeed common to all members of species and do really exist, they exist only as components of individual substances, and not in a separate, immaterial realm.

Individual substances are a compound of form and matter, and the one cannot exist without the other. Our knowledge of objects depends entirely on our sensory experience of them, and humans and animals have the same sensory experience (subject to variations due to differences in sense organs). What distinguishes human from animal knowledge is that the human intellect can abstract the form from the sensory data, whereas animals cannot. Aristotle failed to explain why only humans can abstract forms, but the answer is probably the unsatisfactory one that forms are intellectual in nature, and all the remaining properties of substances are material. Animals are wholly material, and can recognize only material properties, whereas humans have an intellectual component, which can recognize intellectual as well as material properties. So, although Aristotle brought Plato's forms down to earth, he still retained the primitive idea that like is known by like: the material element knows the matter, and the intellectual element knows the immaterial form. And even if we accept his contrast between the intellect and the senses, it is hard to make sense of the idea that an intellectual form is a component of a material object.

The second theory of universals is conceptualism. According to conceptualism, there are no universal entities in the world, such as Plato's or Aristotle's forms. Everything that exists is an individual object, and only concepts in human minds are universals. So individuals belong to the same species, not because of their relation to a universal form of the species, but because they come under the same concept in people's minds. This theory eliminates the mysterious forms, and it also avoids the assumption that there is a fixed number of different kinds of thing laid down for all time. But although the theory has greater flexibility, it does not mean that our classifications of things into species are entirely subjective. Our general concepts are general because they apply to properties or groups of properties which are genuinely identical or similar in a number of things, and absent from other things. Objects made of solid gold have different shapes, sizes and functions, but they all have the same atomic weight, and roughly the same colour; and even if no two cats are exactly identical, they all have more in common with each other than they have with any dog. Nevertheless, each occurrence of each property is individual in itself, and only concepts embrace all these individual properties universally.

The third theory of universals is nominalism (from the Latin *nomen*, meaning a name). According to this theory, only names or words are universal. However, there are different versions of nominalism. The most extreme is that, since there is nothing general in reality corresponding to general terms, they are meaningless. It is, of course, highly paradoxical to deny that words like 'gold' and 'cat' have any meaning, and it is unfortunate that none of the writings of alleged extreme nominalists have survived. The Greek philosopher Cratylus (a younger contemporary of Socrates) was said to have become so sceptical about the meaningfulness of language that he gave up speaking altogether. In the middle ages, the French philosopher Jean Roscelin (c. 1050–1120) was accused by St Anselm (1033–1109), Archbishop of Canterbury, of holding that general terms were 'mere spoken puffs of air' (in Anselm's book *On Faith in the Trinity and on the Incarnation of the Word, against the Blasphemies of Roscelin*). In our own age, some post-modernist philosophers have written at length on the ultimate meaninglessness of language.

A less extreme version of nominalism holds that there are no real kinds in nature, and that the only thing that members of the same species have in common is that they have the same name. In other words, classification is a purely human activity, and it is entirely arbitrary how things are divided into different classes. However, it is still paradoxical to deny that our general terms have any objective basis – it is not a mere human whim that gold is really different from silver, and that cats are different from dogs.

The mildest version of nominalism is like conceptualism, except that it makes language prior to concepts. General terms are names of things rather than of concepts, and whatever is in our minds when we talk about general classes is only of psychological interest. We classify things as belonging to the same kind on the basis of shared properties; but there are indefinitely many ways of doing this. It is ultimately up to us which features we consider significant, and different societies might classify things in different ways.

We now come to the question of where Hobbes stands on the issue of universals. He claims to be a nominalist. In the *Elements of Law*, chapter 5, Article 6, 'Universals do not exist in the real world', he says:

> The fact that one name is universal to many things has been the reason why people think that the things themselves are universal. They seriously maintain that, in addition to Peter and John, and all other individual human beings who exist, who have existed, or who will exist in the world, there is also something else which we call 'human', *viz* human being in general. But they make the mistake of taking the universal, or general name, for the thing it signifies. If you commissioned an artist to do you a picture of a person, which is as much as to say of a person in general, you would mean no more than that the artist should choose anyone they liked to draw. This would have to be someone who exists, or has existed, or might exist in the future – none of which are universal. But if you asked them to draw a portrait of the king, or any other individual person, you would be restricting the artist to the one individual you yourself had chosen. It is therefore obvious that there is nothing universal apart from names. They are therefore also called 'indefinite' names, since we do not ourselves determine any individual, but leave them to be applied to an individual by the hearer. By contrast, a singular name is determined or restricted to just one of the many things it signifies; as when we say 'this man' while pointing to him, or giving him his proper name, or by some other such means.

Hobbes's analysis of what is wrong with realism is very acute, and characteristically based on an argument to do with the nature of language. His point is that realists assume that words have meaning only if there is a distinct, real entity corresponding to them. The word 'human' does not mean the same as 'Peter' or 'John', therefore there must be a separate humanity-in-general to which it refers. But Hobbes points out that the difference between general and singular names is not that general names refer to general entities; rather, they refer indefinitely to a range of individuals.

What is missing in this passage is an explanation of how the word 'human' refers indefinitely to Peter, John, etc., but not to other individual things, such as Peter's dog, or John's hat. The answer is, of course, that universal names are given meaning by being defined, and the definition specifies the properties that are common to all members of the class of which it is the name. But this calls into question the extent to which Hobbes is actually a nominalist. For example, he is perfectly happy to accept the traditional, Aristotelian definition of a human as a rational animal. So he agrees that some animals objectively have the property of rationality, and others do not: human beings really are human beings. To this extent he is a realist. But he differs from Aristotle in at least two ways. First, he does not believe that there are immaterial forms, distinct from the properties of material bodies – all that exist are bodies and their properties. Second, he does not believe that there is a finite number of forms corresponding to the natural species of things. Humans can define any class of things they like into existence, provided there is some common property. For instance, we could invent a word for animals with orange fur, which would cut across conventional distinctions between lions, tigers, cats and so on.

We next need to consider how Hobbes's nominalism is distinct from conceptualism. Nominalism collapses into conceptualism if a philosopher holds that we have general concepts in the mind corresponding to general linguistic terms. There is one passage in Hobbes where he seems to be arguing that we could have general concepts, and use them for reasoning, even if we had no language at all. This is in *On Body*, chapter 1, article 3: 'On mental reasoning':

However, there is a problem over how we are able to add and subtract by purely mental reasoning, when thinking non-verbally . . . Suppose someone sees something obscurely from a great distance. Even if no words have yet been imposed on things, they will have the same idea of the thing as the idea by virtue of which they would call it a 'body', now that we have imposed names on things. Coming nearer, they will see the same thing somehow changing its position, and they will have a new idea of it, by virtue of which they now call such a thing 'animated'. Then, standing close up, they would see its shape, hear its voice, and perceive other things which are signs of a rational mind, and would have yet a third idea, even if it had not yet been given a name – that is, the same idea on account of which we say something is 'rational'. Finally, when they conceive the whole thing as a unity, which is now seen completely and distinctly, this last idea is a compound of the preceding ones. This is how the mind makes compounds of the above ideas, in the same order as the individual names body, animated, and rational are in language compounded into the single name rational-animated-body, or human being.

This passage is completely unsatisfactory as an account of how we acquire general concepts, since it confuses the fact that some properties of a thing are more easily detectible from a distance than others, with the fact that some properties are more general than others. But there is no logical reason why the most salient properties of a thing should be the most general. I suspect that Hobbes has been misled by saying that we see things 'more obscurely' at a distance, and their detailed properties only when they are close up. He conflates the obscurity of the distant object with the lack of specificity of a general concept, and the details which can be discerned when an object is close with highly specific properties common to only a small number of objects.

Not only is this theory unsatisfactory in itself, but it is inconsistent with what Hobbes says elsewhere about what we have in our minds when we entertain a general term. In the very next chapter of *On Body* (chapter 2 section 9), he writes:

So the name 'universal' is not the name of some *thing* existing in the universe, nor of an idea, nor of some phantasm formed in the mind, but it is always the name of some word or name. So that when it is said that an animal, or a rock, or an image, or anything else is a universal, this is not to be understood as meaning that any person, rock, etc. was, is, or could be universal; but only that the *words* 'animal', 'rock', etc. are universal names, i.e. names common to a number of things; and the concepts in the mind corresponding to them are images or phantasms of individual animals or other things. Hence, in order for us to understand the force of 'universal', there is no need for any faculty other than the imagination, by which we remember that words of that sort have brought into the mind sometimes one thing, sometimes another.

Here Hobbes is absolutely explicit that only names are universal, and any images in our minds accompanying our words are images of particular things. You could say that it is like illustrations in a novel: the meaning of the story is determined by the words of the text, and for every incident illustrated, there is an indefinite number of possible particular drawings consistent with the text. By giving primacy to names rather than concepts, Hobbes is clearly a nominalist rather than a conceptualist.

vii. TRUTHS

Some philosophers have held that truths exist independently of the existence of the material universe or of human beings. It seems quite plausible to say that it was true that dinosaurs existed millions of years before human beings evolved and developed languages in which it is possible to say 'Dinosaurs existed' or the equivalent. Similarly, if there comes a time when the whole material universe is annihilated, it will still be eternally true that the universe ceased to exist on such-and-such a date.

Hobbes rejects this entirely, because he holds that truth is a property of propositions, not of things. The proposition 'Dinosaurs existed' is true because dinosaurs did in fact exist, but it is the proposition that is true, not the dinosaurs. So, there cannot be any truth without propositions. And propositions do not exist independently of sentences made up of words in human languages. The primary reality is linguistic communities using sentences consisting of arbitrarily defined words to exchange information, and the only reason why we use more abstract terms such as 'concept' or 'proposition' is to indicate that different words and sequences of words in different languages have the same meaning. So we say that 'house' in English and 'maison' in French denote the same concept, because an English person and a French person would point to the same range of objects on being asked to indicate what a 'house' or a 'maison' is. Similarly, on being asked to evaluate the truth of the sentences 'My house is large' and 'Ma maison est grande', the English person and the French person would give the same answer. But the concepts of a concept and of a proposition are parasitic on the concepts of a word and of a sentence. If there were only one language, there could be words and sentences without concepts or propositions; but there cannot be concepts or propositions without human users of language.

Thus, in *On Body* chapter 3 section 8 ('True and False belong to language, not things'), Hobbes writes:

> It follows from this that there is no place for truth and falsehood except in living beings which have the use of language. If animals which lack language see the image of a person in a mirror, they can be affected in the same way as if they had seen the actual person, and therefore cringe or fawn at it in vain. However, they do not take the thing as true or false, but only as similar and in this they are not deceived. So just as humans owe good reasoning to properly understood language, they owe their errors to badly understood language. And just as the human race alone is graced by philosophy, only humans are subject to the shame of absurd dogmas . . . It can also be deduced from this, that the first truths of all arose from the wills of those who first imposed names on things, or accepted names imposed by others. For example, it is true that *humans are animals*, just because of the arbitrary decision to impose those two names on one and the same thing.

In this passage, Hobbes runs together three distinction themes of his philosophy. One is that humans are distinguished from animals only by their capacity for language. The second is that humans can be worse off than animals, because we are subject to absurd beliefs which cannot arise without language (for example no animals believe in astrology, whereas many humans do). The third theme, which is the one relevant here, is that the concept of truth has no application outside the use of human language, and that language is an entirely human artefact. Without humans, there would be no truths.

viii. INFINITY

Another area of controversy was whether or not there exist infinite numbers, or beings that are either infinitely large or infinitely small. On the whole, mathematicians who believe that there are immaterial entities corresponding to mathematical terms and concepts are happy to accept the existence of actual infinities, whereas those who tie mathematics closely to the world of experience tend to reject them. Hobbes is one of the latter.

Hobbes made a conventional contrast between a 'potential' and a 'completed' or 'actual' infinity. A potential infinity means simply that however far you go, you can always go further, whereas a completed infinity means that there actually exist infinite numbers, or infinitely many things, or infinitely long distances, or infinite stretches of time, or infinitely small particles. He accepted the former, but was distinctly dubious about the latter. In *On Body* chapter 7 section 12, he writes:

> A space or time is . . . *potentially infinite* if there can be a larger number of such paces or hours than any given number. It should be noted that even in the case of potentially infinite space or time, although more paces or hours can be counted than any specifiable number, their number will still be finite, since every number is finite.

Here he seems to be saying that a potential infinity is not an actual infinity, because if it has a number that number will be finite, – even if it is a larger number than humans can possibly count up to. That it is a human limitation is confirmed by his later remark in chapter 26 section 1:

> . . . you will never be able to carry on to eternity. Eventually you will have to give up through exhaustion, and you will not even know whether you could have got any further or not.

Just as there is no infinitely large number, similarly there are no infinitely small particles. In *On Body* chapter 7 section 13, he says:

> It is usually said that space and time are infinitely divisible. But this should not be taken as meaning that some infinite or eternal division has actually taken place. The meaning of the statement is better expressed as follows: *whatever is divided is divided into parts which can be further divided*; or alternatively, *there is no minimum divisible*; or as most geometricians put it, *it is always possible to specify a smaller quantity than any given quantity.*

For Hobbes, the *word* 'infinite' is unproblematic, because we can give it a consistent definition and use it in practice. As he says in *On Body* chapter 5 section 5:

> 'Number is infinite' is false, since there is no infinite number, but only the name or word 'number'. When it is not backed up by any specific number in the mind, the *name* is called 'in*def*inite', but there is no such thing as an *in*finite number.

What we cannot have is any *conception* of a completed infinity. As he says in *Leviathan* chapter 3 (CL 15):

> Whatever we imagine is finite. Consequently there is no idea or concept which can be conjured up by the word 'infinite'. The human mind cannot accommodate an image of infinite size; nor can it conceive infinite speed, infinite force, infinite time, or infinite power. When we say that something is 'infinite', all we mean is that we cannot conceive any bounds or limits to the thing concerned, and merely conceive our own impotence . . . Since, as I have said above, anything we conceive has previously been perceived in sensation, human beings cannot have any imagination of a thing which is not perceptible by the senses. Consequently, no-one can conceive anything except as in space, and as having some finite magnitude, and as divisible into parts; nor can anything be conceived as being wholly in different places at the same time; nor can two or more things be conceived as

occupying the same place at the same time. None of these states of affairs ever was or could be given in sensation. They are meaningless verbiage, sanctioned by the authority of various deluded philosophers, or mistaken university professors.

There are really two arguments here, the first of which is a bad one, and the second a good one. The first argument is that, since the human mind is finite, it is too small to contain an infinite concept. This is a bad argument, because it assumes that a concept must itself have the properties it specifies as belonging to the things of which it is the concept. It confuses a mental image of a thing with an abstract specification of the properties a thing must have in order to be of a certain kind. If Hobbes had stuck to his principle that only names with their definitions can be infinite, he would have been on much firmer ground. As it happens, Descartes made much the same mistake as Hobbes on this point, because he argued that since the concept of God as an infinite being was too great for us to have created by ourselves, it must have come from a really existent God.

The second argument is the better one that we can only conceive or imagine what we have experienced. Everything we experience is finite, so we can have no conception of the infinite. This raises the question of whether or not there might actually exist infinite quantities, even if we cannot have any conception of them. In *On Body* chapter 7 section 12, Hobbes dismisses one argument for saying the world must be finite as fallacious, and then says:

> . . . if we ask whether the world is finite or infinite, we have nothing in our minds corresponding to the word 'world', since whatever we imagine is finite simply by virtue of being imagined, whether we count as far as the fixed stars, or to the ninth, the tenth or even the thousandth sphere. The only question is whether God has actually added as much body to body, as we can add space to space.

So, since we can neither experience nor conceive infinity, the question of whether or not there are any infinite quantities is not a scientific or philosophical question, but a theological one. As he says in *On Body* chapter 26 section 1:

> Consequently, questions about the magnitude and origin of the world are not to be decided by philosophers, but by those who have legal responsibility for managing the worship of God. . . . What is absolutely unforgivable is that the people who argue so absurdly are not mere amateurs, but geometricians, who set themselves up as strict judges of other people's demonstrations, even beyond their sphere of competence. The reason is because, once they become entangled by the words 'infinite' and 'eternal', which are not backed up by any idea of anything in the mind, apart from its own lack of comprehension, then either they have to say something absurd, or they have to shut up (which is even less to their liking) . . . So I deliberately pass over questions about the infinite and the eternal. I am satisfied with what the Holy Scriptures teach about the magnitude and origin of the world, and I accept them, along with the stories of miracles which confirm them, and the traditions of my country, and the respect owed to the law. I now move on to other matters, which it is not sacrilegious to argue about.

Whatever Hobbes might actually have believed about actual infinities, he was more conscious than most in his day and age of the incredible smallness of the parts of natural objects, and of the enormous size of the universe. In *On Body* chapter 27 section 1, he speculates that there are creatures too small to be seen through any microscope, despite his preposterous claim that there were already microscopes with a resolution of over a hundred thousand times. He then continues:

> Nor is the smallness of some bodies any more surprising than the enormous size of others. The same infinite power can make things infinitely larger as well as infinitely smaller. It is equally within the power of the Author of Nature, both to bring it about that the great orbit (namely that of which the radius extends from the earth to the sun) is like a point in relation to the distance

of the sun from the fixed stars, and, on the other hand, to make a body so small, that it is smaller than anything visible, by the same proportion.

ix. GEOMETRY

We have already seen how Hobbes reduced arithmetic to the process of counting by means of an arbitrarily decided sequence of names of numbers, without presupposing that numbers had any independent existence. Geometry was more of a problem, because Hobbes wanted geometrical truths to be true of the real world of material objects, and not of some extra-terrestrial realm of perfect circles, triangles, cubes and other figures. It was a problem because, whereas natural numbers can be exactly instantiated in groups of objects, certain geometrical quantities cannot.

In particular, it has been known since the time of Pythagoras that certain quantities which have a clear abstract definition cannot be physically instantiated. For example, if you have a right-angled triangle of which two of the sides are one unit in length, then the third side will be $\sqrt{2}$, which has an infinite number of decimal places (1.4142135623730950488016887242209 ... and so on). This means that if the first two sides are made up of atoms, however small, then the third side cannot be constructed with atoms of the same size, since it will either be slightly too long or slightly too short. Similarly, if you have a circle with a diameter of one unit, its circumference will be π, or 3.1415926535897932384626433383279 ... and so on. Again, if the diameter is made of up atoms, however small, then the circumference cannot be constructed with atoms of the same size, since it will either be slightly too long or slightly too short. Numbers such as $\sqrt{2}$ and π are known as 'irrational numbers', because there is no finite ratio between them and natural numbers like 1, 2 or 3.

This raises a serious question as to how geometry relates to reality. The solution adopted by Pythagoras and Plato was to say that the figures of which geometry is true, such as right-angled triangles and circles, exist only in an immaterial, ideal realm, and that physical triangles and circles are merely approximations to them. We can never construct a perfect triangle or circle, although we can

approach the ideal as closely as our technology allows us, and geometrical formulae are applicable to reality with a corresponding
level of accuracy.

This approach was not available to Hobbes, because he denied
the existence of immaterial objects and abstract ideas. Ultimately,
geometry had to be about actually existing material objects. It is
quite a challenge to devise a philosophical theory which reconciles
the necessary truth of geometry with a materialist view of the world
and a broadly empiricist account of how we know it (a challenge
which was later central to Kant's philosophy). Unfortunately,
Hobbes took the wrong route, and in effect denied that there were
any irrational numbers, so that geometry could apply directly to the
real world. What Hobbes did was to claim that he could square
the circle – that is to say that, using the methods of Euclidean
geometry, he could construct a square that had exactly the same
area as that of a given circle. This is in fact impossible, and Hobbes's
repeated publications purporting to show that he had squared the
circle were riddled with errors, and they did immense damage to his
reputation as one of the leaders of the modernist revolution in
philosophy and science. He was refuted in detail by a number of
mathematicians, but instead of accepting that he was wrong, he
persisted in writing books on squaring the circle, and in heaping
scorn on his critics.

Nevertheless, his insistence that geometry must be about the real
world was perfectly sensible in principle. We use circular wheels to
measure linear distances without worrying about the incom-
mensurability of π. We find it no more difficult to draw triangles
with sides of $1:1:\sqrt{2}$ than ones with sides of 3:4:5. So, despite the
existence of irrational numbers, geometry must in some sense be
about the world of our experience. Hobbes felt strongly that geometers were simply wrong to hold that their science was true only of
an abstract, immaterial realm separate from the material world.
They were wrong in the same way as scholastic metaphysicians who
believed in immaterial entities. And just as Hobbes was willing to
write off the universities as filled with credulous and incompetent
philosophers (as he frequently did), he was equally willing to write
off their mathematicians.

What Hobbes failed to realize was that, while university philosophers remained wedded to traditional scholasticism, the study of
mathematics had been radically transformed since his days as a
student. Then, the only method recognized as deductively valid was
the synthetic method of the ancient Greeks, in which one moved
from the simplest definitions and axioms to complex theorems.
Their approach to geometry was also 'synthetic' in the sense of
'putting together' simple components such as straight lines and
curves in order to construct complex diagrams. Consequently there
was nothing in Greek geometry which could not be represented
visually in the real world of experience.

A revolutionary break from this approach was made by François
Viète (1540–1603), who championed an analytic rather than a synthetic method. His method was further developed by Descartes,
whose analytic geometry entitles him to be called the father of
modern mathematics as much as the father of modern philosophy.
The essence of the analytic method is that it uses algebra rather
than visual diagrams to define geometrical figures. For example, the
general formula for a circle is $x^2 + y^2 = k$. By giving particular values
to the variables and using Cartesian co-ordinates, a particular circle
can be represented diagrammatically. But the geometrical equation
is the primary entity, and the drawn diagram is no more than one
particular way of illustrating it. For Descartes it was crucial that
truths known by reason should be divorced from the illusions of
sense and imagination. Even a disembodied mind with no way of
representing things spatiotemporally would be able to appreciate
geometrical truths expressed algebraically.

Of course, this was anathema to Hobbes, for whom all truth had
to relate to the material world. In *On Body* chapter 20 section 6, he
explicitly rejects Viète's analytic approach:

> Nor do the rules of analysis make a good geometrician; whereas
> synthesis does, when it begins with the elements themselves, and
> accompanies the elements with their logical use. The correct
> method for teaching geometry is the synthetic method, as
> systematically laid down by Euclid. If you have Euclid as your
> master, you can become a geometrician without Viète. Although

Viète was clearly an admirable geometrician, if you have Viète as your master without Euclid, you cannot become a geometrician.

Later in the same article he makes it clear that the problem with the analytic method is that it is divorced from reality:

It is wholly inappropriate for either learning or teaching geometry, and its only use is for keeping a quick and brief record of geometrical discoveries. Even though symbols make it easier to go through a long chain of propositions, I doubt that the process should be considered of much use, since it takes place without any ideas of the things themselves.

In the twenty-first century, it is still a controversial issue whether mathematics is ultimately about the world of material objects or about some separate abstract and timeless realm. Hobbes was absolutely committed to the former view, against the prevailing fashion. It is a pity that he spoilt his case by committing serious errors in his attempts to square the circle; but that does not invalidate his philosophical position that all truths are true of the material world.

x. CAUSE

Following Aristotle (*Physics* chapter 2 section 3), the scholastic philosophers held that there were four kinds of cause, or ways of explaining why a thing is as it is. These causes complemented each other, and all four were required in order to provide a complete explanation.

The first type of cause was the *material* cause, or the kind of matter a thing was made of. For example, of two otherwise identical statues, one might be made of stone and the other of wood. So part of the reason why a stone statue is as it is, and is different from a wooden statue, is because it is made of stone, not of wood.

The second type of cause was the *formal* cause, or the form by virtue of which an individual belongs to the same species as other individuals with the same form, and is different from individuals of other species. Thus, cats have certain physical and behavioural characteristics which are different from those of dogs, and which they pass on to their offspring.

The third type of cause was the *efficient* cause, or that which brought a thing into being. All Aristotle's examples are of human agents such as the sculptor who carves a statue out of stone or wood – though he probably also had in mind the God who created all the kinds of thing not created by humans. In scholastic philosophy, the concept of the efficient cause was extended to inanimate objects which brought about changes in things, such as the wind rustling the leaves of a tree, or ocean waves eroding a cliff.

The fourth type of cause was the *final* cause, or the purpose for which something was created (from the Latin *fines*, meaning 'purpose'). This might be a human purpose, or a divine purpose, or a more abstract striving towards the fulfilment of a particular nature. For example, the whole point of an acorn is to become an oak. The way it develops is driven by this goal, and you have no scientific understanding of its nature unless you know this crucial fact about it.

The Aristotelian theory of four causes was by no means the only theory in play in the early seventeenth century. Outside the university system, the humanist movement of the Renaissance had generated a large number of classical scholars, who were either independently wealthy, or were supported by wealthy patrons (indeed Hobbes himself had many of the characteristics of the Renaissance scholar, since he was supported by the Devonshires, and much of his output consisted in translations of Greek literature). These intellectuals were responsible for bringing to light a far wider range of ancient philosophical theories and concepts than the narrow Aristotelian diet of the universities. In particular, many were captivated by the worldview of philosophers who had developed Plato's philosophy in a far more mystical direction than Plato himself ever intended. They believed that things on earth (the microcosm) mirrored and were controlled by things in the heavens (the macrocosm) – a belief in astrology being just one aspect of this. They also believed that the powers of natural substances depended on 'occult virtues' or hidden powers, which could be unearthed by people with the right sort of wisdom, or 'natural magicians' as they sometimes styled themselves.

Needless to say, Hobbes and the other proponents of the new philosophy rejected out of hand the approach of the Neoplatonists and natural magicians as superstitious nonsense. As for the Aristotelian four causes, Hobbes did not dismiss them completely, but he redefined them to suit his own purposes. Thus, in *On Body* chapter 9 section 4, he writes:

> When an effect is produced, the totality of the accidents required for the effect which are in the agent or agents is called its *efficient cause*. The totality of those which are in the patient when an effect is produced is usually called the *material cause* ... The efficient cause and the material cause are partial causes, or parts of the cause which we called *complete* just above. From this it immediately follows that the effect which we expect when there are appropriate agents can be frustrated for lack of an appropriate patient, and when there is an appropriate patient, it can be frustrated for lack of appropriate agents.

I shall say more about how Hobbes changes the meaning of 'efficient cause' below. Here he has no use for the traditional concept of a material cause, because he does not recognize that there are different kinds of matter at all. There is simply one homogeneous body, which differs in different places because of the structure and motions of its parts and the perceptible accidents they give rise to. Instead, he makes a relative distinction between the conditions in the body which acts on another (the agent), and the conditions in the body which is acted on (the patient), both of which are required for a given effect to be brought about. For example, if one glass ball strikes a stationary one (the efficient cause), the second one will move off in the same direction only if it is strong to withstand the impact (the material cause). That the distinction is not an absolute one is shown by the fact that in many cases, both objects involved in an interaction are equally active.

In *On Body* chapter 10 section 7, Hobbes turns to formal and final causes:

In addition to efficient and material causes, metaphysicians list two other types of cause, namely *essence* (which some call the *formal cause*), and *purpose*, or *final cause*. However, both are really efficient causes. The *essence* of a thing is said to be its cause, as if *being rational* were the *cause of a human being*. But this is unintelligible, since it is the same as if we said that *being a human* was the cause of a human, which is an abuse of language. On the other hand, knowledge of a thing's essence is the cause of knowledge of the *thing*, since if I already know that something is rational, I know from this that it is a human. But the way in which it is a cause makes it nothing other than an efficient cause. *Final causes* have no place except in relation to things which have sense and will; and I shall show that these are also efficient causes in the proper place.

Hobbes's defence of formal causes is disingenuous, because he rejects the Aristotelian concepts as 'unintelligible', and it is a strange use of language to say that the essence or definition of a thing is the efficient cause of knowledge of it. His real point is that the concept of a formal cause has no function.

He is on much firmer ground when he says that final causes apply only to things which have sense and will. Because of the doctrine that everything has a final cause, previous accounts of nature attributed purposes to everything: heavy objects fall because they are striving to find their proper place; acorns strive to become oak trees; nature abhors a vacuum – and so on. Although the denial of final causes is one of the defining features of the modern revolution in philosophy, it is interesting how the language of purposefulness often creeps back into scientific explanations nearly four centuries later, as if there is a deep human need to see events in nature as analogous to human activity.

When he says that even in the case of sentient beings, final causes are really efficient causes, he means that voluntary acts can be explained as the effects of purely mechanical processes in the animal body. I shall come back to this in the next chapter.

To return to efficient causes, Hobbes, along with the other moderns, had a very restricted view of what counted as an efficient cause. For the scholastics and the Renaissance humanists, just about anything could count as an efficient cause. But for Hobbes, the only efficient cause, and indeed the only cause at all, was one piece of matter pushing another piece of matter. This is often referred to as *mechanical* causation, and the science of mechanics provides the mathematical laws governing all the ways in which bodies of different shapes, sizes and weights interact with each other at different speeds. The mechanical worldview, to which Hobbes adhered, was the view that nature consists of nothing other than material particles in motion, and that all phenomena can be reduced to them. In Hobbes's day, this was more a vision than a reality, and it was only the end of the seventeenth century that saw a mature science of mechanics at the hands of Leibniz and Newton.

Although the modern philosophers should be applauded for their desire to give the simplest possible account of nature, and to confine it to quantities which could be treated mathematically, it must be noted that the earliest attempts were grossly *over*simplified. In particular, what is missing is any concept of an *attractive* force. It is easy to understand why they believed that repulsion, or pushing away, is the basic force in nature. For example, if you have an object on a table, say a mug, you can easily push it away from you with your hand. And if you take your hand away from it, the mug stays where it is, and it does not follow your hand. If you want to bring it towards you, you have to put your hand behind the mug and push it towards you. Things like magnets seemed very mysterious, because of their apparent power to exert an attractive force on iron (though on nothing else).

What they overlooked was that there are many other attractive forces in nature, which cannot plausibly be explained in terms of pushing. Thus, if the mug were covered in glue, I would be able to drag it towards me. Alternatively, I could tie a piece of string to it and pull the string. But no sensible account can be given of how the material particles constituting the string, or those constituting the mug, can hold together despite contrary forces acting on them, if the only forces are repulsive rather than attractive.

Another example is the gravitational force keeping the planets in orbit round the sun. Descartes tried to explain it as really a kind of pushing. He held that space was full of ether, consisting of tiny material particles. By spinning, the sun set up vortices in the ether, rather like water round the plug hole in a bath. The planets were pushed round by the vortices, like ping pong balls in the bathwater. When Newton formulated his theory of universal gravitation a few years after Hobbes's death, he was attacked by philosophers such as Leibniz for bringing back the 'occult forces' of the mediaevals. And Newton himself was very defensive about attractive force: he said its effects were observable in experience, but he was not going to invent any hypotheses about what it was or how it worked.

Hobbes is absolutely explicit that 'all pulling is pushing', which is the title of *On Body* chapter 22 section 12:

> Another distinction between kinds of motion is that between pushing and *pulling*. As I have already defined it, pushing is when that which is moved is in front of that which moves it. By contrast, *pulling* is when the mover is in front of the moved. However, if you consider more carefully, you will see that pulling is really pushing. If you consider two parts of a hard body, the one in front pushes before it the medium in which the motion takes place, and the part it pushes pushes another part, and this pushes another one, and so on. In this action, assuming there is no vacuum, it is necessarily the case that, since the pushing is continuous (i.e. the medium closes up round the object as it goes through), that which is doing the moving is behind the part which originally seemed to be pulled rather than pushed. So since that which is pulled is now in front of the body by which it is moved, it is pushed, not pulled.

Hobbes's idea seems to be that if you pull something through a fluid medium, such as water or the ether, the surrounding particles rush in to the back of the object to avoid the occurrence of a vacuum, and thus push it forward. But while it is true that there will be some such effect, Hobbes overlooks the fact that it does not replace but merely supplements the primary force pulling the object through the medium, which remains unexplained. An adequate account of nature must include attractive as well as repulsive forces.

xi. CONATION

Hobbes held that all change is ultimately a change in motion. In *On Body* chapter 9 section 9, he says:

> . . . change is nothing other than the motion of the parts of the body undergoing change. Firstly, we do not say that anything has changed, except when it appears to our senses differently from how it appeared before. Secondly, both these appearances are effects produced in the sentient being . . .

And he goes on to argue that effects can only be the effects of motions in the body. In other words, all the perceived qualities of things and all the phenomena of nature are really nothing but motions.

From this he draws the more radical conclusion that everything is always in motion. As he says in *Ten Dialogues* chapter 2:

> I say, then, that in the first place you must enquire thoroughly into the nature of motion, since the differences between one phantasm and another, or (which is the same thing) between one phenomenon of nature and another, all have one universal efficient cause, namely the differences between one motion and another. If all the things in the world were absolutely at rest, there could be no difference between one phantasm and another, and living creatures would be without any sensation of objects; which is hardly less than to be dead.

Obviously things are not always in the motion in the sense of moving from one position to another. What Hobbes means is that the invisibly small parts of things are constantly vibrating, and causing the qualities we perceive in them. If these motions ceased, the material world would be no more than an undifferentiated mass. For virtually all of Hobbes's contemporaries, matter was essentially inert, and could only move when acted on by another body. But for Hobbes, the invisible parts of every piece of matter were in ceaseless motion. This anticipates the twentieth-century physics, according to which the temperature of a body is a function of the rate of motion of its molecules, and subatomic particles spin round the nucleus of an atom.

Another, and equally important, aspect of these imperceptible motions is Hobbes's theory of *conation* (or *conatus* in Latin, and *endeavour* in Hobbes's English). For the ancients, one of the defining characteristics of an animal was that it was capable of initiating motion. So, if there is a dog sleeping beside a stone, at some time the dog will wake up and walk away; but the stone will stay where it is unless it is moved by the dog or by some other force. Hobbes was anxious to underplay the differences between animate and inanimate objects, just as he underplayed the differences between humans and other animals. Moreover, he was well aware that there are many events in nature which are not caused by animals – wind, rain, waves, earthquakes and so on. If these are to be explained naturally, there must be some way in which they can be set off without the intervention of supernatural beings.

In modern physics, we have concepts such as those of force, energy and power for explaining how an inanimate object can initiate motion. In Hobbes's day, these had not yet been developed in any scientifically rigorous way, and his concept of conation was a highly original attempt at developing a concept of what initiates motion. As we saw in Chapter 2, Hobbes held that genuine science must be deductive. In other words, there cannot be anything in the effect that is not already implicit in the cause. Consequently, the cause of motion cannot be of an entirely different nature from motion itself. On the other hand, it must be different enough for the explanation not to be circular, or assuming what is to be explained in the explanation. Hobbes tries to resolve this dilemma by defining conation as what we would now describe as an 'infinitesimal' motion. As he says in *On Body* chapter 15 section 2:

> I shall define conation as a motion through space and time which is less than any given quantity . . . in other words, it is a motion through a point. In order to explain this definition, I must remind you that by 'point' I do not mean that which has no quantity, or which cannot conceivably be divided, since there is

no such thing in the real world. Rather, it is that the quantity of which is entirely disregarded, in other words, that of which neither the quantity nor any part of it enters into the calculation for the purposes of demonstration. So a point should not be taken as indivisible, but as undivided. In the same way, an *instant* should be taken as an undivided period of time, and not as an indivisible one.

This is a remarkably clear definition of infinitesimal motion, as well as of points and instants as infinitesimals rather than as having no dimensions at all (which Hobbes rightly regarded as physically impossible). However, making the cause of motion an infinitesimal motion does not actually solve the problem of how motion can arise from that which is not itself motion. Ultimately it is still a motion, and a vanishingly small one at that. Nevertheless, as we shall see later, the concept of conation was very useful to Hobbes in his account of human nature, and of crucial importance for the future development of mathematical physics.

xii. DETERMINISM

Determinism is the view that the universe necessarily evolves in the way it does, and at no point could it ever evolve differently than the way it actually does. Hobbes is effectively committed to determinism both because of his claim that scientific knowledge is acquired by deduction, and because of his definition of a cause. In *On Body* chapter 9 section 3, he says:

So the causes of all effects consist in specific accidents of the agents and the patient. When they are all present, the effect is produced; and if any one them is absent, the effect is not produced. But an accident, whether of the agent or of the patient, *without which* the effect *cannot be produced*, is called *the cause 'without which not', and which is necessary by hypothesis*; and *the prerequisite* for the effect to be produced. *A cause* without qualification, or *a complete cause is the totality of all the accidents, both of the agents (however many there may be) and of the patient, such that assuming all to be present, it is inconceivable that the effect should not be produced together with it; and assuming one of them to be absent, it is inconceivable that that the effect should be produced.*

This is actually a very strong version of determinism. Most determinists have held that the evolution of the universe is contingent: that is to say that, even though its history is determined and cannot be altered, it is perfectly possible to *imagine* a change in the laws of nature so that it could develop differently. But in the above passage, Hobbes explicitly denies that, given a complete set of causes, any effect other than the actual one is even conceivable. This is paradoxical, because it seems perfectly possible to imagine all sorts of things happening differently – for example, the sun not rising, or a pile of dry gunpowder not igniting when a match is put to it. I suspect that Hobbes's answer would be to draw a distinction between what can be conceived and what can be imagined. When he discussed angels in Section iii above, he said that we might have an *image* of a pretty little boy with wings, even though angels are strictly inconceivable. Similarly, we might have an *image* of a set of causes having a different effect, but the image would bear no relation to reality as we correctly conceive it.

Another reason for Hobbes's strict determinism is that, along with many of his contemporaries, he made no distinction between logical and physical possibility or impossibility. Nowadays, we distinguish sharply between round squares or married bachelors, which are logically impossible, and flying pigs or 10 metre giants, which contain no logical contradiction, but which are physically impossible. Some philosophers even go so far as to say that there are possible worlds which contain logical possibilities that are impossible in this world. Hobbes would certainly have ridiculed this idea as populating reality with an absurd number of quasi-entities. However, it may be that his failure to recognize unrealized possibilities stems from an understandable feeling that the very notion of the existence of an unactualized entity contains a contradiction. In *On Body* chapter 10 section 4, he defines impossible and possible as follows:

An action is impossible if the full power for producing it will never exist. Given that a full power is one which combines everything which is required for producing an action, if the full power will never exist, one of the necessary requirements for producing the action will always be absent; therefore this action could never be produced – in other words, this action is *impossible*.

A *possible* action is one which is not impossible. Consequently, every possible action will be produced at some time or other; for if it is supposed that it will never be produced, it will never be the case that all the requirements of its production will come together; therefore (by definition) this action is impossible, which is contrary to what was supposed.

So something which never happens is impossible, and something which is possible will either have happened in the past, or will happen in the future.

Traditionally a distinction had been made between what actually happened in the past, what is actually happening in the present, and 'future contingents', or possible events in the future which are not yet known. Obviously Hobbes cannot allow future contingents to be any less necessary than past or present events, and he explains their meaning in *On Body* chapter 10 section 5:

Here you might ask whether so-called future contingents are necessary. My global answer is that everything which happens contingently is contingent upon necessary causes, as I have shown in the previous chapter; and events are called 'contingent' only in relation to other events which they do not depend on. For example, tomorrow's rain will be produced necessarily (i.e. by necessary causes); but we think and say that this rain happens by chance, because we have not yet seen its causes, which already exist. People call something a 'chance' or 'contingent' event when they cannot see through to its necessary cause. They habitually talk about past events in the same way, when they say that it is 'possible' that something did not happen, when they mean that they do not know whether it happened or not.

So every proposition about a future contingent (e.g. 'It will rain tomorrow') or a future non-contingent (e.g. 'The sun will rise tomorrow') is necessarily true or necessarily false. But when we do not yet know scientifically whether a proposition is true or false, we call it 'contingent' on that account – even though its truth does not depend on our scientific knowledge, but on preceding causes.

As on so many occasions, Hobbes gives a linguistic account of the difference between the necessary and the contingent. There is no difference in reality, but we call an event 'contingent' when we have insufficient knowledge of its causes to know whether it will happen or not. And as he had already said in *On Body* chapter 9 section 10:

In relation to their causes, all things happen with equal necessity; for if they did not happen necessarily, they would not have causes – something which is unintelligible in the case of things which have come into being.

In other words, an event which was not necessary would be uncaused, and an uncaused event is impossible, because it would lack the preconditions of its happening.

Another reason for Hobbes's strong determinism is his belief that the universe consists in a holistic, interconnected system. Medieval philosophers tended to consider small chains of events in isolation from one another. Consequently, it would make no difference to a particular chain of events if there were random events elsewhere in the world. But if, as Hobbes held, everything is interconnected, then broken links would damage the systematic unity of the whole. As he says in *Of Liberty and Necessity* (p. 246):

Nor does the co-operation of all causes consist in one simple chain or concatenation, but in an innumerable number of chains. They are not joined together at every point, but they are in the first link, which is God Almighty. Consequently, the whole cause of an event does not always depend on one single chain, but on many together . . .

Admittedly, Hobbes is not as thoroughgoing a holist as later philosophers who believed that everything was always interconnected with everything else. But his claim that the whole cause of an event sometimes involves many causal chains together is certainly a move in that direction. Given that, as we have already seen, he held that the universe was filled with a vibrating ether transmitting light and other forces to great distances, it is somewhat surprising that he did not make more of the interconnectedness of the universe.

Finally, there is a question whether Hobbes's insistence that there is only one way in which the universe could possibly evolve is consistent with the point he made in *On Body* chapter 25 section 1 (see Chapter 2 section x above), that God could have created the world in one of a number of different possible ways, and that we cannot know which when reasoning back from effects to causes. On the face of it, these two positions are inconsistent. But if confronted with this apparent contradiction, Hobbes would probably reply that he is merely pointing out the extent of human ignorance. Just us we can describe events as contingent when we do not know their causes, we can say that God could have created the world in different ways when we do not know which he chose. From a divine perspective, there was presumably only one rational possible choice. But, we humans have no insight at all into the inscrutable divine understanding.

CHAPTER 4

THE HUMAN BEING

i. INTRODUCTION

I have already covered a number of aspects of Hobbes's account of the nature of the human being: perception, knowledge, language and the absence of an immaterial soul. In this chapter, I shall consider humans as active agents in the world.

In the previous chapter, on Hobbes's materialism, nearly all the references were naturally to *On Body*, the first part of his grand trilogy, *The Elements of Philosophy*. You might expect most of the references in this chapter to be to the second part of his trilogy, *On the Human Being*. In fact, *On the Human Being*, which was the last part to be published (when Hobbes was 70), comes as a great disappointment. It is relatively short, and it contains virtually no new material. By no stretch of the imagination does it constitute a systematic treatise on the human being to compare with the detailed, radical and innovative *On Body* and *On the Citizen*. The first half covers much the same ground as his early *Optical Treatise*, and the rest is a shortened version of the relevant *Leviathan*, Part I: *On the Human Being*. It would be a mistake to attribute the shortcomings of this work to Hobbes's age, because he continued to publish prolifically for the next 20 years. Rather, it seems that he simply had nothing more to say, and he cobbled a book together from his earlier writings in order to complete his trilogy. Even Part I of *Leviathan* is far from systematic, and much of it consists of definitions of human emotions (often quite contentious), and mini-essays on the human condition.

ii. APPETITE AND AVERSION

In *Leviathan* chapter 6, Hobbes distinguishes between vital and animal motions, and he argues that the latter are caused by conations (CL 27–28):

> Animals have two kinds of motions which are exclusive to them. One is *vital* motion, which starts at conception, and continues throughout life without interruption – for example, the motion of the blood, the pulse, breathing, digestion, nutrition, or excretion, none of which require the help of the imagination. The other is called 'animal' or 'voluntary' motion – for example, walking, talking, or moving one's arms, which are preceded by a thought in the mind. As has already been said (in chapters 1 and 2), sensation is a motion in the sense organs and internal parts of the human body brought about by objects which are seen, heard, etc.; whereas phantasy is the after-effect of the same motion when sensation has ceased. Walking, talking, and other such voluntary motions always depend on some preceding thought, such as 'where to' 'by what route', or 'what.' Consequently, it is obvious that phantasy is the first internal beginning of all voluntary motions. Some might deny that there is any motion at all when the thing in motion is invisible, or the distance through which it moves is too small to be sensible; but this does not mean that there are no motions of this sort. However small the distance, something moving through a greater distance, of which the small distance is a part, will necessarily also pass through the latter. These small beginnings of motion, which take place within the human body before they become apparent as walking, talking, hitting, or other visible actions, are called 'conations'.

A number of points need to be noted here. First, although the distinction between vital and voluntary motions was quite traditional, Hobbes was very radical in identifying *all* voluntary motions with animal motions. He leaves absolutely no room for there to be an additional rational soul controlling the body through its own acts of will. The contrast that springs to mind is with Descartes, for whom the will was one of the two functions of the immaterial soul. Even so, the contrast is not as stark as might be supposed, since Descartes held that the human body normally runs on automatic pilot, so to speak, and it is only when the soul wishes to counter bodily inclinations for moral reasons that it intervenes. As Descartes says in his *Treatise on the Human Being*, p. 185:

> But in my opinion, the most noteworthy consequence of memory [as a natural faculty of the brain] consists in the fact that this machine [the human body], without the presence of any soul and simply by virtue of the dispositions natural to it, is capable of imitating all the movements which real people, or even other similar machines, will make with a soul present.

The second point to note in the Hobbes passage is that his argument about motion is rather confused. What he seems to mean is that an image or phantasy consists of a motion in the brain or sense organs, even if we are not conscious of any motion. For example, if we are staring at a motionless object, we are not aware of anything moving, but in fact the image itself is a rapid motion. Moreover, unlike a physical picture and more like picture on a television screen, it is constantly being refreshed. Since the motion is below the threshold of consciousness, it is in effect an infinitesimal quantity. And by implication, there can be mental events of which we are unconscious.

The third point to note is that conation or endeavour is exactly the same concept as Hobbes used to explain the beginning of motion in inanimate objects. Because of his materialism, there can be no ultimate difference between animate and inanimate matter. Just as inanimate objects can be set in motion by the conations of microscopic parts, the same is true of humans and other animals.

Immediately after this passage, Hobbes introduces the key concepts of appetite and aversion:

When this conation is directed towards its cause, it is called 'appetite' or 'desire' . . . When, on the other hand, the conation is directed away from something, it is called 'aversion'.

These are crucial to Hobbes's theory. To say that an image is a conation which sets the body in motion is a start, but it does not explain the direction in which it moves. As we saw in Chapter 2 section vii, sensations are pleasurable if they aid the vital motions of the body (e.g. by giving us warmth or nourishment), and painful if they impede them (e.g. by damaging bodily tissues). Now he says that we have an impulse towards the object of perception if it is pleasurable, and away from it if it is painful. Obviously, this is too simple an account to explain all human behaviour; but it is a bold first attempt at providing a framework for understanding human action as the outcome of purely physical factors.

iii. GOOD AND EVIL

By definition, what we desire is called 'good', and what we avoid is called 'evil'. Some things, like food, are innately desirable. But for the most part, different people like and dislike different things, depending on their constitutions and experience. Even one and the same person might like different things at different times. As Hobbes says in chapter 6 (CL 28):

And because the constitution of the human body is constantly changing, it is impossible for the same things always to give rise to the same appetites and aversions. Much less can everyone have the same appetite for one and the same object.

He recognizes that there are also things to which we are indifferent, considering them to be neither good nor evil. Oddly, in the English version, he describes this attitude as 'contempt' rather than indifference.

The outcome is that nothing is absolutely good or evil, but only in relation to the desires and aversions of individuals (CL 28–29):

Whatever is the object of anyone's appetite is what they for their part call 'good'. Similarly, anything that is the cause of aversion or hatred they call 'evil'. And anything they are indifferent to, they call 'worthless'. For the words 'good', 'evil', and 'worthless' are always understood as relative to the person who uses them, since nothing is good, evil, or worthless in itself. Nor can any universal criterion for their application be derived from the nature of their objects, but only from the nature of the person using them (if in a state of nature), or (if there is a civil society) from the person representing the state, or from someone appointed as an arbiter or judge.

In other words, in a state of nature, where there is no authority to determine what is right or wrong, the terms 'good' and 'evil' have no objective meaning. Things are not good or evil in themselves, but only relative to the preferences of individuals. The consequence is that there is no science of ethics or morality independent of a political and judicial authority which can impose a set of values. Nor are there any objective moral values by which the laws of a state can by evaluated. Without the state, there is nothing other than the preferences of individuals.

The ancient philosophers had different theories about the *summum bonum*, or the highest good to be achieved in this life. Hobbes had two reasons for rejecting the whole concept of a *summum bonum*. One was, as we have just seen, that what is good is different for different individuals, and there is no single good in itself. The other is more interesting. This is that if you achieve the highest good, then you have nothing left to strive for. But since the human being is nothing other than a lump of matter characterized by a complex of conations, if you have achieved the highest good, then you have no more conations, and you are just dead matter. As he says in chapter 6 (CL 34):

Perpetual success in obtaining the things we want is what is called 'happiness'. I mean happiness in the present life. For there is no perpetual tranquillity of the mind as long as we live, because life itself is motion, and humans can no more live without desire, and fear, and other emotions, than without sensations.

And in chapter 11 (CL 57):

> It must be understood that in this life happiness does not consist in tranquillity or repose of the mind. For the *ultimate goal* and the *highest good* which the ancient writers on ethics spoke about have no place in the present life. Nor could anyone whose desires had come to an end be alive, any more than one who had lost all sensation and memory.

Hobbes allows that life after death may be closer to the ancient ideal of tranquillity, but this is something about which we can have no knowledge.

iv. DELIBERATION AND WILL

Hobbes totally rejected any idea that specifically human actions are the result of an act of will by an immaterial soul. Nevertheless, he still had to account for the fact that human beings do not merely react to external forces as is the case with inanimate objects, but can initiate actions from their own resources. He ascribes this to a process which he calls 'deliberation'. In *Leviathan* chapter 6, he describes it as follows (CL 33):

> It is called 'deliberation', when, in the human mind, appetite and aversion, or hope and fear about one and the same thing arise alternately. One after the other there come into the mind the good and bad consequences of doing it or not doing it. Consequently, at one moment we are motivated towards it, and at another against it; at one moment we are hopeful, and at another we are fearful. Deliberation is the totality of these emotions taken together, and it lasts until the course of action is either carried out or rejected . . .

> . . . Deliberation is said to come to an end when the object of deliberation is either put into effect or made impossible, because up to that point we retain the liberty of doing it or not doing it, according to our own judgment.

Hobbes is implicitly distinguishing between situations in which we react to events without thought (for example defending ourselves against a sudden attack), and situations where we apply our reasoning to what we should do, and then act on the outcome. The latter correspond to cases where other philosophers would have said that our actions are the outcome of an act of will by the immaterial soul. For Hobbes, however, there is nothing more than a purely natural alternation between appetite and aversion, until one side or the other wins. His characterization of thoughtful as contrasted with instinctive decision-making echoes Plato's definition of thinking as 'the soul's silent inner dialogue with itself' (*Sophist* 263e). This is a pretty accurate description of what goes on in our minds when we are thinking about what decision to make – we think of considerations in favour of a particular action, and then of considerations against it, and after a certain amount of to-ing and fro-ing, we opt for one or the other.

Hobbes's claim that, as long as we are still deliberating, we retain the liberty of acting or not is rather disingenuous. He is, of course, correct to say that once we have come to a decision, we are no longer free, since we are committed to the course we have decided on. But to claim that until that happens we are still free by-passes all the difficult issues of the freedom of the will, which we shall come to shortly.

In the same passage, he makes two other claims. First, he says:

> Another reason why it is called 'deliberation' is because it puts an end to our liberty of doing or not doing something.

This must be a Hobbesian joke. He would surely have known that the Latin *deliberatio* comes from the word *libra*, meaning a balance or weighing scales, so that deliberation is a process of weighing the pros and cons of an action in a balance which will ultimately come down on one side or the other (as in the statue of Justice on the Old Bailey). Here he pretends it comes from the negative prefix *de-* and *liberatio* which means making free – hence putting an end to freedom.

The second claim is that:

> This alternation between appetite and aversion, etc. is common
> to humans and other animals; for lower animals also deliberate.

This is a perfectly fair observation. For example, animals can dither
as to whether to fight or run away from another animal, or whether
or not to leap to somewhere dangerous; and it is reasonable to
assume that there is something non-verbal going on in their brains,
analogous to what goes on in ours when we deliberate. But Hobbes
is very radical in saying that humans and other animals are identical
in this respect, since the ability to think about what action to take
was almost universally held to be one of the things that distinguished humans from animals as involving the power of reasoning.
It is just one more example of Hobbes's playing down the differences, so as to remove any grounds for saying that specifically
human abilities can be explained only by possession of an immaterial, rational soul.

We now come to Hobbes's definition of the will. After discussing
deliberation, Hobbes writes (CL 33):

> In deliberation, the last appetite immediately before the action
> (or avoidance of it) deliberated about is the *will*; and I say it is the
> act of willing not a faculty of willing. From which it follows that
> animals are also endowed with will, because they deliberate. The
> scholastic definition of the will, namely *that the will is rational
> appetite*, is illegitimate. For if that is what it was, there could
> never be any voluntary act that went against reason. For a volun-
> tary act is one which arises from the will, and nothing else.

The significance of the scholastic definition is that the will is a faculty of the rational soul which differentiates humans from animals.
Here, Hobbes rejects the definition on a number of grounds: first, it
is not a faculty at all, but an action – namely that of making a
decision which results in our doing or not doing what we were deliberating about. Secondly, it is something we have in common with
animals, so it has nothing to do with reason. And thirdly, for an
action to be voluntary has nothing to do with whether it is rational
or not, since we sometimes voluntarily do things that are irrational.

The upshot of Hobbes's minimalist account of the will is that there is no additional factor mediating between our appetites or aversions and what we actually do. Our senses provide us with images or phantasms, and depending on whether their objects help or hinder out vital functions, we are either attracted towards them or repelled away from them. Sometimes we act spontaneously, and on other occasions we first deliberate. Deliberation consists in alternate appetite and aversion, and the last one (called the will) determines what action we take.

v. FREEDOM AND DETERMINISM

Hobbes says relatively little about freedom and determinism in his main writings. He defines what he means by 'voluntary' or free action in *Elements of Law* chapter 12 section 3:

> *Voluntary* actions and failures to act are those which have their beginning in the will. All others are *involuntary* or *mixed*. Voluntary actions are those which are done because of appetite or fear. Involuntary actions are those which are done by the necessity of nature, as when you do good or harm to someone else because you have been pushed, or have fallen. Mixed actions participate of both, as when a man being taken to prison is pulled along against his will, but voluntarily walks upright for fear of being dragged along the ground: in walking to the prison, his *walking* is voluntary, but his walking *to the prison* is involuntary. The case of a man who throws his goods out of a ship into the sea in order to save his person is an example of an entirely voluntary action, since there is nothing there which is involuntary, apart from the difficulty of the choice. But this is not the man's action, but the action of the winds. What he himself does is no more against his will, than to flee from danger is against the will of someone who sees no other way of saving themselves.

All this is admirably clear, and it would be acceptable to almost any philosopher, but for Hobbes's definition of the will. The problem is that, although some actions do indeed proceed from the will and others not, the will itself, as the last appetite or aversion, does not proceed from the will but from perceptions of the external world and the disposition of the individual human body. It therefore follows that even voluntary actions ultimately follow from the 'necessity of nature'. Thus, in *On Body* chapter 25 section 13, he writes:

> Nor is the freedom of willing to do something or not to do it any greater in humans than in other animals. When a being has an appetite, the complete cause of the appetite will have preceded it, and therefore . . . the appetition itself could not have failed to follow, in other words, it followed necessarily. So if freedom means freedom from necessity, then it is incompatible with the will of humans as well as that of other animals. But if by 'liberty' we mean the capacity, not of *willing*, but of *doing* what we will, then liberty in that sense can be accepted in both cases; and when it is present, it is present equally in both humans and other animals.

Hobbes's point here is that every event has a necessary complete cause, and if the causes are insufficient, then it cannot happen. This is as true of human actions as of anything else in the universe. Consequently, freedom cannot mean freedom from necessity. What it does mean is freedom to do what we will, even if what we will is necessitated. This still leaves scope for a meaningful distinction between voluntary and involuntary actions. For example, I might will to walk out of my room, and do so freely. On the other hand, someone may have locked the door, and I am not free to leave it. In the former case I am free, and in the latter case I am not.

In *On the Human Being*, chapter 11 section 2, Hobbes addresses the illogicality of those who maintain that, in order for our will to be free, we must freely will what we will:

> So, as with sensation, the causes of appetite and avoidance, or pleasure and pain, are the actual objects of sensation. From this it follows that neither our appetite nor our avoidance is the cause of our desiring or avoiding this or that – in other words, that we do not have an appetite for something because we will to do so,

since will itself is an appetite. Similarly, we do not avoid some-thing because of a contrary will, but because both appetite and avoidance are brought into being by the things themselves which we desire or hate, and there necessarily follows a preconception of the future pleasure or pain from those objects. But what am I saying? Can it really be that we are hungry, and have an appetite for other necessities of life, because we will to be hungry? Can it really be that hunger, thirst, and other desires are voluntary? When people have an appetite towards something, it is certainly possible for their *action* to be free, but not their *appetition*. This is so obvious from anyone's own experience, that I never cease to be amazed how many people fail to understand how it can pos-sibly be the case. When we say that someone has a free choice between doing or not doing something or other, we must always take as understood the qualifying clause 'if they so will;' for it would be absurd to say that someone has a free choice of doing this or that, whether they will it or not.

As Hobbes says, the argument here is drawn from experience. We simply do not will to have certain desires or aversions – we just have them. It could be argued against him that we can in fact desire to have desires. For example, someone might have no motivation to give up smoking, but might wish to have such a motivation, and set about acquiring it by reading anti-smoking propaganda, looking at photographs of diseased lungs and so on. Hobbes's response would be that this person really does desire to give up smoking, but has to use roundabout and necessary causal methods to translate a gener-alized desire into an effective act of will. Elsewhere, in *The Elements of Law* chapter 12 section 5, he provides a more philosophical argument against our being able to control our desires voluntarily:

Appetite, fear, hope, and the other passions are not called 'volun-tary', since they are not the *result* of the will, but they *are* the will; and the will is not voluntary. You can no more say that you will to will, than that you will to will to will, and hence repeat the word 'will' infinitely many times – which is absurd and meaningless.

This is Hobbes's strongest argument against those who maintain that, for an action to be free, it cannot be part of a necessary causal chain, but must be the consequence of a free act of volition. If the free act of volition comes out of the blue, then it is less your own act than if it arose (necessarily) from your own particular nature and circumstances. And if, in order for your will to be free, your volitions have to be the outcome of previous free volitions, then there is an infinite regress. Hobbes's position is that you are what you are for reasons outside your control, but what you are determines your destiny within the constraints imposed by external factors.

I said that Hobbes had little to say about freedom and determinism in his main writings. But two volumes of his complete works are given over to his lifelong dispute with Bishop Bramhall over freedom and determinism and the nature of God. However, neither writer is least persuaded by the other, and they pass each other by in the night. The one new point to arise is that of whether it is possible for us to be anything other than necessitated, given that the universe was created by an all-powerful, all-knowing God. For Hobbes this is not a problem, since he has already accepted that we are necessitated. It causes much greater difficulty for Bramhall, since it is difficult to see how such a God can create us knowing everything we are going to do, without being responsible for what we do. In his replies, Hobbes makes great play of the way Bramhall uses obscure (and for Hobbes meaningless) scholastic terminology in order to get out of the difficulty.

At the end of *The Questions Concerning Liberty, Necessity, and Chance, Clearly Stated and Debated between Dr. Bramhall, Bishop of Derby, and Thomas Hobbes of Malmesbury*, No. xxxviii, Hobbes deftly summarizes his position on freedom and determinism:

> What I have maintained is that no-one has his future will in his own present power. It may be changed by others, and by changes in the external world. When it is changed, it is not changed or directed to any determinate object by its own activity. If it is undetermined, then it is not a will at all, because everyone who wills, wills something in particular. Deliberation is common to humans and animals, since it is the last of alternating appetites,

and not an exercise of reasoning. The last act or appetite in deliberation, which is immediately followed by the action, is the only will that can be observed by others, and which alone makes an action voluntary in the eyes of the public. To be free is no more than for a person to do what they want, or not to do it if they do not want to. Consequently, this freedom is the freedom of the individual, and not of the will. The will is not free, but subject to change by the operation of external causes. All external causes depend necessarily on the first eternal cause, God Almighty, who brings about what we will and what we do by secondary causes. Since neither human beings nor anything else can exert causal influences on themselves, it is impossible for anyone to co-operate with God in forming their own will, whether as an active agent, or as God's instrument. Nothing is caused by chance, and nothing happens without a cause, or a combination of causes sufficient to bring it about. Every such cause and combination of causes proceeds from the providence, will, and action of God. Consequently, although I like everyone else call many events *contingent* and say they *happen*, yet because they all had their various sufficient causes, and those causes in turn had their earlier causes, I say they *happen* necessarily. Even though we do not perceive what these causes are, even the most contingent events have causes that are just as necessary as those of the events whose causes we do perceive. If this were not so, they could not possibly be known in advance, as they are by God, who knows everything in advance.

vi. THE EQUALITY OF HUMANS

The two main aspects of a human are intelligence and bodily characteristics. Let us consider intelligence first. In Hobbes's day, it was normal to hold that all human beings were equally intelligent, at least in potential, because they all had qualitatively identical rational, immaterial souls. But Hobbes did not believe in immaterial souls, so he did not have this particular ground for holding that all humans were born equal. You might expect him to say (as some modern psychologists do) that differences in intelligence are at least partly due to genetically determined differences in the structure of the brain. However, he does not go down this route, because he holds that human brains and sense organs are too similar to each other to explain large differences in intellectual ability.

Hobbes distinguishes between two kinds of intelligence: natural and acquired. Natural intelligence is developed solely by practice and experience, and it consists of two things. These are quickness of the imagination, or the speed with which one thought follows another, and steadiness of concentration on an approved purpose. The extent to which they are developed in any individual depends on differences in temperament. Acquired intelligence depends on explicit training rather than experience, but the extent to which it is developed also depends on temperament. In this, Hobbes takes broadly the same line as modern psychologists who hold that differences in IQ are relatively insignificant, and that the development of intellectual skills depends more on upbringing and aspiration. In the English *Leviathan* chapter 8, he says (CL 40–41):

> As for *acquired intelligence* (I mean acquired by method and instruction), there is only reason, which depends on the right use of language, and produces scientific knowledge . . .
>
> The causes of this difference in intelligence lie in people's temperaments; and differences in temperament depend partly on different bodily constitutions and partly on different upbringings. For if the difference depended on the structure of the brain and the sense organs, whether outer or inner, people would differ as much in their sight, hearing, and other senses as they do in their imaginations and preferences . . .
>
> The temperaments that are the main cause of differences in intelligence are principally a greater or lesser desire for power, wealth, knowledge and fame.

Hobbes comes back to differences in intelligence in *Leviathan* chapter 13, and here he downplays the differences between one person and another (CL 74–75):

I now turn to intellectual abilities. But here I exclude techniques depending on words, that is, the general rules of the sciences, which few possess and only in very few areas, because they are not innate in us, and they are not acquired by practical wisdom without deliberate effort. I say that there is even more equality between people in intellectual ability than in physical strength. This is because all practical wisdom arises from experience, and nature bestows practical wisdom on everyone in proportion to the amount of time and mental effort they have devoted to things. What makes such equality seem doubtful is only the opinion of those who overestimate themselves. For nearly everyone believes they are much wiser than any ordinary person – that is, much wiser than anyone else, apart from a few people they respect because of their celebrity, or because they have the same opinions as themselves. For human nature is such that, although we might admit that some people are more eloquent or more learned than ourselves, we never accept that anyone is wiser than ourselves. For each of us observes our own intelligence from close-to, and that of others from a distance. But for our present purposes, it is the strongest argument for the equality of intelligence, that everyone is satisfied with what they have.

I do not believe that Hobbes meant this last argument seriously. He is, of course, right that it is very difficult for someone of a certain level of intelligence to imagine what it is like to have a higher order of intelligence. But to argue that everyone is equally intelligent because no-one complains of lack of intelligence is wrong to the point of absurdity. The premise is false, because many people are aware that others are wiser than themselves, and the inference is invalid because, even if some people believe that no-one can be wiser than themselves, they could simply be mistaken. Hobbes must have meant it as a joke, and, uncharacteristically, it was not even original, because the joke had already been made by Cicero in antiquity, and it had also been borrowed without acknowledgment by Descartes in the opening sentence of the *Discourse on the Method*:

Of all things in the world, good sense is the most fairly distributed, since everyone thinks they are so well provided with it, that even those who are the most difficult to please in every other respect, do not usually want more of it than they already have.

As for bodily characteristics, Hobbes argues that, although some people are clearly stronger than others, even the physically strong are vulnerable to attack by the weak. At the beginning of *Leviathan* chapter 13, he writes (CL 74):

> Nature has made people so equal among themselves in the powers of both body and mind, that, although some are superior to others in strength or intelligence, when everything is taken into account, the difference is not great enough to guarantee one person a good which someone else has not an equal hope of obtaining. As for strength of the body, you will rarely come across anyone so weak that they cannot kill the strongest of people by guile, or by collusion with others in equal danger.

The point of Hobbes's emphasis on equality is that, in a state of nature, no-one is safe from anyone else.

vii. THE STATE OF NATURE

The state of nature is a state in which there is no civil authority. Without an authority, no-one has any rights, or, to put it another way, everyone has an equal right to everything. So when two people want the same thing, they become enemies. As Hobbes says in *Leviathan* chapter 13 (CL 75):

> Arising from this natural equality, everyone has a hope of acquiring whatever they desire. So whenever two people want the same thing, but only one of them can have it, they become each other's enemy; and in order to achieve their goal (which is self preservation), they try to overpower or kill each other. Therefore if someone is minded to attack their neighbour, and the only deterrent is the strength of a single person, whenever someone possesses a better piece of land, and sows and plants crops, and builds a house on it, then they can expect others to band together

and deprive them, not only of all the fruits of their labour, but even of their life and liberty. And the same will happen to the usurpers at the hands of people stronger than themselves.

Hobbes is not quite logical here, because the fact that two people are not much different in strength is irrelevant to his example. If there is a fight between two individuals, then a difference in strength or cleverness is just what makes the difference between victory and defeat. But if a band of people attack an individual, it hardly matters whether that individual is weak or strong. But this does not affect Hobbes's essential point, which is that without a central authority, everyone is in fear of everyone else, and there is no point in trying to build a better life if anything you produce is going to be stolen. As he puts it in the same chapter, the state of nature is a state of constant war (CL 76):

> Therefore in human nature there are three principal causes of strife: competition, defence, and self-esteem; of which the first aims at property, the second at security, and the third at respect . . .
>
> So it is obvious that, as long as there is no coercive authority, the condition of humans is what I have called war between everyone and everyone else. For the nature of war does not consist in an actual battle, but in a period of time during which the willingness to fight things out is generally understood.

It is crucial for Hobbes's later argument for an absolute authority that nothing is worse than a state of war. However, awful an absolute dictatorship might be, complete anarchy is even worse. So he paints the gloomiest possible picture of the state of nature (CL 76):

> Therefore whatever naturally arises from a war of everyone against everyone necessarily attaches to the human condition when there is no security other than that which can be expected from each individual's strength and intelligence. In such a condition, there is no place for hard work, because there is no profit from it. So there is no cultivation of the land, no navigation, no

comfortable buildings, no machinery for moving things which require more than human power, no knowledge of geography, no means of telling the time, no arts, and no society. Instead, what is most serious of all, there is fear and a permanent danger of violent death, and the life of people is solitary, poor, brutish and short.

This last phrase is the most quoted of Hobbes's pronouncements, and in the English *Leviathan* it is slightly longer as: 'And the life of man, solitary, poor, nasty, brutish, and short.' Perhaps he could not work out how to translate 'nasty' into Latin. This sound-bite has also been widely misunderstood, and a 'Hobbesian' view of society has been assumed to be just as he describes the state of nature. But this is to turn Hobbes upside down, because, as should be evident from quoting him in context, he uses the dreadfulness of the state of nature as his fundamental argument for creating a state with a single, absolute authority. There is nothing Hobbesian about a life that is solitary, poor, brutish and short, because his whole purpose is to explain scientifically why it is not.

Hobbes sometimes talks as if there was a historic period when there was no civil authority anywhere, and then nation states came into being at various times. However, it is quite unnecessary for his argument that there ever was a state of nature: it is enough to be able to imagine what it would be like if there were no authority, or to consider what happens when there is a partial breakdown in authority, as in the Civil War. Thus, in chapter 13 of the English *Leviathan*, Hobbes writes (CL 77):

It might perhaps be thought that there never was a time when there was a state of war such as this. And I believe that it was never universally so over the whole world. But there are many places where people live like this now. For the savages in many parts of America have no government at all (apart from the government of small families, in which peace depends solely on their having the same desires), and they live today in the brutish manner I described above. In any case, you can see what sort of life there would be where there was no common authority to fear, by the way of life which people who have formerly lived under a peaceful government usually degenerate into in a civil war.

Hobbes is unduly negative about the quality of life of native Americans, and primitive peoples in general. However, this does not necessary falsify his thesis, because it could be that at any level of development, there will be sufficient central authority to prevent the worst excesses of a state of nature. Even in the English Civil War, the breakdown of authority and personal security was only partial, and it neither proves nor disproves what would happen if the collapse of authority were total.

viii. NATURAL LAWS

So how do we get out of a state of nature? Two essential ingredients (although these are not the only ones) are a desire for peace, and a number of principles known by reason, which Hobbes calls natural laws, or laws of nature. At the end of *Leviathan* chapter 13, he says (CL 78):

> The emotions by which people can be led to peace are fear (and especially fear of a violent death), a desire for things necessary for the good life, and a hope of obtaining them by hard work. And reason suggests certain principles, which are natural laws.

The concept of natural law, or of fundamental moral principles known directly by reason, was quite commonplace in Hobbes's day. But it sits oddly in Hobbes's philosophy, because he has already said that in a state of nature, what is good or evil is relative to the desires and aversions of individuals, and has nothing to do with objective reason. Other philosophers held that natural laws were ordained by God, and that he had implanted in our souls innate ides of these laws. This explanation was not available to Hobbes, because he rejected both souls and innate ideas. The clue to what is going on here is to be found in the last paragraph of chapter 15 (CL 100):

These dictates of reason have wrongly been called laws, because they are only theorems about the things which promote the preservation of people's lives. Strictly speaking, a law is the edict of a ruler . . .

In the English version, he says that they are properly called laws if they are considered as delivered by the word of God. But this is disingenuous, because Hobbes accepted only the Bible as the word of God, and his natural laws are not in it. The significant word is the word 'theorem', which is a geometrical term. In geometry, theorems are propositions derived from more fundamental axioms, but it seems likely that Hobbes is thinking of axioms here rather than theorems. We have already seen that Hobbes believed that he was the founder of the new science of politics, which would be developed by logical deduction from a priori axioms, just like Euclid's geometry. In order to achieve this he needs some axioms, and these are supplied by his laws of nature. But, as throughout Hobbes's philosophy, there is a tension between his empiricist insistence that all the material for our knowledge comes from sense experience, and his rationalist insistence that we have knowledge of necessary truths, even if they ultimately depend only on the definitions of terms we have arbitrarily imposed.

Hobbes distinguishes between a law of nature and a right of nature. There is only one right of nature, which Hobbes specifies as follows at the beginning of *Leviathan* chapter 14 (CL 79):

The right of nature is the liberty which everyone has of using their own power for the preservation of their nature, and consequently of doing everything which seems to them to promote it.

This right justifies each individual's selfish behaviour in the state of nature, and as we shall see, it persists until it is renounced. But it is also this right that gives rise to the first law of nature (CL 80):

The human condition . . . is a condition of war of everyone against everyone, and hence everyone is governed by their own reason. And because there is nothing which might not at some time be useful for defending their life against an enemy, it follows that in the state of nature everyone has a right to everything, even including other people's bodies. Therefore as long as that right persists, no-one, however strong, can have any security. So it is a precept or general rule of reason that *peace is to be sought as long as there is hope of obtaining it; and when there is no hope of having it, it is legitimate to seek and use any means of defence whatever.*

In other words, Hobbes takes it as a fundamental axiom that we should strive for peace, since it is obviously better to live in security than to be constantly in fear of one's life. However, if there is no such hope, we retain all the unlimited rights we have in a state of nature to defend ourselves. He then moves directly on to the second law of nature (CL 80):

From this first law of nature follows the second, that, *as long as the foreseeable outcome is peace and their own security, and provided others are willing to do the same, everyone should give up their right to all things, and be content with the same liberty as they are willing to concede to others.* For a state of war remains as long as everyone retains the right to do what they want. But if the others refuse to lay down their right to everything, then no-one is obliged to lay down their right. For that would be considered as exposing themselves as a prey for others rather than pursuing peace.

As the primary axioms for a science of politics, these are remarkably hedged with qualifications. We should seek peace, but only if there is a good chance of its happening. We should give up our rights in order to attain peace, but only if others do so as well. This is because truths of reason are essentially hypothetical: *if* all the preconditions are present, *then* the conclusion will follow. But if the preconditions are not present, we are back to square one with the state of nature, and the laws of nature simply do not apply. What is missing is a central authority to impose peace, and this will be the topic of the next chapter.

In the meantime, Hobbes devotes the whole of chapters 15–19 subordinate laws of nature, which together constitute an a priori ethical system. It might seem puzzling that Hobbes should produce an a priori ethical system at all, given that, in a state of nature, 'good' means no more than what each individual wants, and in a civil society, it means whatever is ordained by the sovereign. There appears to be no room for ethics as well. But this is to misunderstand Hobbes's purpose. As I said above, he saw himself as the founder of a *science* of politics, and the theorems of this science would be specific rules for preserving the peace enjoined by the first two laws of nature. Thus, at the end of chapter 15, Hobbes sums up the rationale for the subordinate laws (CL 100):

> As long as private individuals are the measure of good and evil, everyone is in a state of war of all against all. Therefore everyone agrees that peace is a good thing, and strives after it. Consequently it cannot be denied that the means for securing peace are necessarily good. And these means are the above-mentioned justice, gratitude, modesty, fairness, and the other laws of nature. Therefore they are morally good, or virtues; and their opposites are evil, that is, vices. But the science of virtues and vices is moral philosophy. And therefore the doctrine of the laws of nature is the true ethics.

So, the true ethics is the science of the virtues required in order to preserve peace. This is not to say that everyone will be virtuous, or even that all the virtues will be enshrined in the civil laws of any given state. But the more closely a society conforms to the laws of nature, the more likely it is that peace will be preserved.

CHAPTER 5

SOCIETY

i. A SCIENCE OF SOCIETY

In the Epistle Dedicatory to *On Body*, Hobbes runs through a list of people who were the first to set various areas of human knowledge on the path of a genuine science. The ancient Greeks founded geometry; Nicolas Copernicus (1473–1543) founded astronomy; Galileo Galilei (1564–1642) founded mechanics and William Harvey (1578–1657) founded medicine. Then Hobbes proudly adds himself as the founder of political science:

> But political philosophy is even more of a novelty, since it is no older than my own book *On the Citizen* (I am provoked into saying this, so that my detractors will know how little they have achieved).

As we saw in Chapter 2 section ix above, Hobbes held that we can have genuinely scientific knowledge only of things we ourselves create: we know their causes because we ourselves have caused them. The consequence (which seems paradoxical to the modern mind) is that the only genuine sciences are geometry, because we ourselves generate geometrical figures; engineering, because we construct machines and politics, because civil society is a human artefact. Physical science, or what we normally call 'science', is not genuinely scientific for Hobbes, because we do not know how God created natural objects. So, by his own standards, we can accept that

Hobbes was the first political philosopher to maintain that politics is a science in the same sense that geometry is a science, even if we do not agree that he was ultimately successful in this project. Nevertheless, his claim to be a major innovator in political theory has been more than amply vindicated by his place in history.

Hobbes could simply have said that the evolution of civil society from a state of nature was obviously brought about by the actions of people who saw that civil society was preferable to a state of nature. However, in the very first paragraph of the Introduction to *Leviathan*, he draws an elaborate analogy between God's creation of humans, and humans' creation of civil society. This was to emphasize that human action in creating the state was equivalent to divine action in creating the human body; and since the state was a human creation, we have scientific knowledge of how it functions. Indeed, the state can be seen as modelled on the body, which gives us insights into how the state functions. The passage is worth quoting in full (CL 3–4):

Human art can imitate nature (that is, the divine art by which God created and governs the world) to such an extent, that it can, among other things, produce an artificial animal. Life is nothing other than the motion of the limbs, which has its internal source in some principal part of the body. So what is to prevent us from saying that all automata (that is, all machines which get their motion from springs and wheels arranged inside them, like clocks) also have an artificial life within themselves? What is the heart other than a spring; what are sinews other than strings; and what are joints other than so many wheels, which impart motion to the whole body in accordance with the designer's intentions? Art does not merely imitate animals, but the noblest animal of all, namely the human being. That great Leviathan, which is called the 'state', is the product of art, and is an artificial person; even though it is much larger and more powerful than the natural persons who invented it for their own protection and security. In this artificial person, the individual who holds sovereign power corresponds to the soul, which gives life and motion to the whole body; magistrates and officials are

its artificial limbs; rewards and punishments, which are the pre-
rogative of the sovereign power, and by which each member is
stimulated to perform its function, are its sinews, which do the
same in a natural body; the wealth of individual people corresponds to its strength; the security of the people corresponds to its
business; advisers, who bring what needs to be known to the attention of the supreme power, correspond to its memory; equity and
laws correspond to its artificial reason; agreement is health; dis-
sension is disease; and civil war is death. Finally, the contracts
which bind the parts of this political body together imitate the
divine words 'Let it be', or 'Let us create a human being,' which
God uttered in the beginning, when he created the world.

A number of features in this passage are worthy of comment. First,
Hobbes stresses, as always that the human body is nothing other
than a physical machine, driven by springs and wheels, like a clock
(a modern Hobbesian would draw an analogy with modern technology such as a computer). Given that there is no magic 'spark
of life', there is no reason in principle, other than its immense
complexity, why we should not be able to create a living human
body. But even though in practice we cannot create living human
beings, we can create automata with artificial life. When he uses the
word 'automaton', he does not mean to *contrast* an automaton with
a living organism; rather, he means *anything* that is capable of
independent action, whether created by us or generated in the normal course of nature. Similarly, when he uses the word 'artificial', he
does not mean that artificial life is fake, as we might say that a robot
is not really alive; rather, he means that automata are genuinely
alive, but that the life has been given to them by what he calls
'human art' as contrasted with divine art. So the state (which he
also calls 'civil society' or 'the commonwealth') is a living organism
created by humans. Comparing the state, or 'body politic', to the
human body is by no means original to Hobbes – it was a recurrent
theme from ancient Greece onwards. Hobbes's originality consists
in his stressing that the state is a human artefact, and drawing the
conclusion that we can have scientific knowledge of it because we
have created it ourselves.

The second point to note is that what finally creates the state is the making of a contract. Hobbes compares this with the creative power of God's words when he brought humans into being. In Genesis 1, most of God's creative acts are represented as following directly from his words, so that his words are the creative acts themselves – for example: 'And God said, Let there be light; and there was light.' In the creation of humans this is less explicit: 'And God said, Let us make man in our image, after our likeness . . . So God created man in his own image, in the image of God created he him . . .'

Nevertheless, Hobbes was fully aware of a crucial point about language which remained unnoticed until the twentieth century, namely that its functions are not limited to the recording and communication of thoughts, but it can change the world. Nowadays we talk about 'performative utterances', to use the terminology of J. L. Austin (1911–1960), who used examples like 'I do thee wed' in a marriage ceremony, which have the effect of creating a marriage. Similarly, Hobbes saw that the form of words used in agreeing a contract created a state of affairs which did not exist previously. And in some cases, a contract could actually create a new institution, with a life of its own, such as the civil state.

The third point is the oddity of Hobbes's calling the state 'Leviathan'. In the passage quoted, he makes it clear that the state is analogous to a super person, with the sovereign as its soul. As we shall see, this analogy is already stretched, because he later allows that the sovereign could be a collective body, such as Parliament, and not just an individual king or queen; and we have already seen that Hobbes did not believe in souls. However, Hobbes's central point remains that the body politic is an organism under the total control of a single authority. This position is graphically illustrated on the title page of the first edition, which has a picture of the king guarding over the town and country of England, with his body consisting of the mass of citizens.

But why Leviathan? There are a number of references to the sea monster Leviathan and the land monster Behemoth in the Bible, especially the detailed descriptions in Job 40–41. Hobbes used both for titles of his works, *Behemoth* being the title of his dialogue on the history of the civil war. While it seems reasonable to name a work on the civil war after a great monster, it seems less reasonable to name a work on the state which is the bulwark against civil war after another monster. But in fact the description in Job does not imply that Leviathan is in any way evil, but only describes his power. The message is that we should be in awe of Leviathan, but not hate him. The title page includes a quotation from Job 41.24 in the Latin Vulgate edition of the Bible, and 41.33 in the King James version: 'Upon earth there is not his like, who is made without fear.' And there are other verses that anticipate some things that Hobbes says about the relation between subjects and the sovereign such as that it is impossible for there to be a covenant between them. For a fundamentalist Christian like Hobbes, who saw the authority of the Bible as the only legitimate supplement to human reason in arriving at the truth, Job 41 was actually a good choice.

ii. THE MAKING OF THE SOCIAL CONTRACT

Hobbes's theory of the social contract did not come entirely out of the blue. Historians of philosophy have found antecedents in earlier philosophers going as far back as Plato. However, Hobbes was the first to formulate a fully systematic social contract theory.

We have seen that it was contracts that brought the Leviathan of civil society to life, and that without a central authority, no one had any duty to obey the laws of nature. So we now need to consider the nature of the original contract which brings it into being. Hobbes describes it as follows in *Leviathan* chapter 17 (CL 109):

There is only one way of establishing a common power to defend people both from external attack and from harming each other, so that they can feed themselves by their own hard work and the products of the earth, and live contentedly. This is for each person to transfer all their power and strength to one individual or assembly, so that the wills of all are reduced to a single will. In other words, for one individual or assembly to take on the person of every individual, and for everyone to accept that they are the authors of all the actions performed by that person, and to submit their wills to the will and judgment of that person. This is something more than just consent or agreement. For there is a genuine unification of all into a single person, brought about by the contract between everyone and everyone else. It is as if everyone said to everyone else, 'I surrender my authority and my right of ruling myself to this individual (or to this assembly), on condition that you also surrender your authority and your right of ruling yourself to the same individual or assembly.' When this is done, the multitude becomes a single person, and is called a state or commonwealth.

There are a number of points here. First, when Hobbes talks of a 'person', he means this in the sense of a *legal* person, which includes not just human beings, but any corporation legally entitled to own property, make contracts and so on. The state is certainly a person in this sense. Nevertheless, as we have seen from the illustration on the title page, Hobbes may also be thinking of 'person' in the normal sense of the term, since the drawing portrays the state as the body of the sovereign, made up of all the citizens. This is consistent with the practice at the time of identifying the sovereign with the state. Thus, Shakespeare often refers to kings as 'England', and Louis XIV of France is notorious for having (allegedly) said 'L'état c'est moi', or 'The state is me'.

Second, Hobbes talks throughout as if the state is an actual, living being, which is brought into existence through the social contract. But how literally does he mean this? Obviously he does not mean that a new physical object has been created. But there is a problem over how real it can be, given Hobbes's materialist thesis that only physical objects exist. There are two possible solutions. One is to say that the state is indeed a physical object consisting of the totality of citizens. What the social contract has done is to change its properties from being an aggregate of individuals at war with one another, to being an organic, co-operative whole that is greater than the sum of its parts. No new physical entity has been generated, but a real difference has been made to what already existed. The other solution is to say that Hobbes already recognizes that there are things about which we can make true statements that are not themselves physical objects, but are parasitic upon physical objects for their existence. In his discussion of language, he distinguished between 'names of the first intention', which are names of physical objects and their properties, and 'names of the second intention', which are names of names. So, for example, nouns and verbs really exist as linguistic items, even though they are not physical, like words existing as marks on paper or vibrations in the air. Similarly, it could be argued that although the state is not a physical object, yet it exists as surely as physical objects do, because it is created and kept in being as an institution by the beliefs and actions of human beings. And just as physical objects can be destroyed by being dissolved into their component parts, so the state (and other human institutions) can be destroyed when the relevant beliefs, contracts and behaviour break down. And this is what happens when there is a civil war.

The third point about the above passage is that Hobbes uses his very strong thesis that the citizens become a single person in order to claim that everyone is the author of that person's actions. By 'author', he means someone who owns or gives their authority for an action. Later, he draws the consequence that it is absurd for any citizen to disagree with any of the actions of their sovereign, because they themselves are the authors of those actions, and therefore they are contracting themselves it they disagree with them. However, this argument is invalid. At one level, it is perfectly reasonable to say that, if citizens have voluntarily handed over to the sovereign the right to make decisions on their behalf, then they have to accept those decisions whether they like them or not. But it is quite a different matter to say that citizens are contradicting themselves if they disagree with a decision. Elsewhere, Hobbes accepts that people may not like some of what the sovereign decrees, but they should comfort themselves with the thought that a state of nature would be far worse.

The fourth point is that the people contract with each other, and not with the sovereign. This is a crucial feature of the contact for establishing the absolute nature of the sovereign's rule. If there were a contract between the people and the sovereign, then the people would have the right to rebel if the sovereign did not adhere to the contract, and the consequence would be civil war and a return to the state of nature. Similarly, the contract is a one-off event. Once the people have renounced their rights, they cannot negotiate a new contract, because it is no longer in their gift, any more than people can renegotiate the price of property they have already sold. As he says in *Leviathan* chapter 18 (CL 110–111):

> Therefore those who are already citizens of a state cannot enter into a new social contract which obliges them to transfer its sovereignty to someone else, or to obey someone else in any matter without the permission of the sovereign. Consequently, those who are citizens of a monarchy cannot, without the permission of the monarch or any other citizen, legally reject the monarchy, nor return to the license of a state of nature.

iii. WAS THE SOCIAL CONTRACT A HISTORICAL EVENT?

Hobbes talks as if there were a time in history when people got together and contracted to leave the state of nature and form a civil society. But as we have already seen, he doubted whether there was actually a pure state of nature, in which case it is doubtful whether people in a state of nature ever got together in order to democratically set up a civil society. Perhaps the closest example is the writing of the constitution of the USA, which was after Hobbes's time, but heavily influenced by his social contract theory as subsequently developed by John Locke (1632–1704). In most cases, constitutions developed over time without any formal social contract.

Another difficulty is that, even if there was an act of signing up to the social contract, no one now alive has done so. Consequently it is hard to see how we can be bound by a contract made by long-dead ancestors. The best that could be said is that the social contract signed away our rights, and that we can no more have them back than we can claim back property sold off by our ancestors. But the mere lack of rights does not explain why the people should be the authors of the sovereign's actions, as Hobbes maintains.

The alternative to seeing the contract as a historical event is to see it as an *implicit* contract which each of us makes by remaining in civil society and enjoying its benefits. This would be similar to Socrates's argument in the *Crito* for not escaping from prison in order to avoid being executed. He said that by staying in Athens rather than emigrating elsewhere, he contracted himself to obey its laws; and if he were condemned to death, he had to accept that. (Though, interestingly, this is the one case where Hobbes would say one is not bound by the contract, since the main rationale for the contract is the preservation of one's life.)

So on this interpretation, we implicitly renounce the rights we would have in the state of nature, in return for the security given to us by civil society. Instead of exacting revenge (if we can) on people who harm us, we leave it to the police and the law; instead of fighting to obtain and keep anything worth having, our possessions are protected by law; instead of being open to rape and pillage by invading foreigners, the state protects us with its army; instead of doing without goods that can be provided only collectively, such as roads and public buildings, they are provided by the state through taxation. If all goes well, we should be much better off with the protection of the state than if we reverted to a state of nature.

So far we have assumed that everyone agrees to the social contract. However, it is an obvious historical fact that there are some people who do very well for themselves in a state of nature. Even today there are a number of failed states with no effective central authority, and where a small number of tribal chieftains, robber barons, gangsters and pirates exert power over the local population, commit serious crimes without any punishment and enrich themselves at the expense of ordinary people. Not only would such people not vote for a social contract, but they would do their utmost to destroy any central authority established by it.

Hobbes recognizes that not everyone would sign up, and he addresses the issue as follows in the English version of *Leviathan* chapter 18 (CL 112):

> Because the majority has declared a sovereign by agreement, those who disagree must now go along with the rest; that is, they must be content to support all the sovereign's actions, or else be justly destroyed by the rest. For if they voluntarily

participated in the assembly, they effectively declared their willingness (and therefore implicitly contracted) to accept what the majority decided. Therefore if they refuse to accept it, or protest against any of the majority decisions, they do so contrary to their covenant, and therefore unjustly. And whether they participated in the assembly or not, and whether their consent was asked or not, they must either submit to its decrees, or be left in the condition of war they were in before. And in this condition, they can be destroyed by anyone whatever, without any injustice.

There are a number of weaknesses in Hobbes's arguments in this passage. First, although it is a commonly accepted democratic principle that a simple majority is sufficient for a decision to be binding, it is by no means universal. There are many institutions where a much larger majority is required on constitutional issues, and in some, such as the Security Council of the United Nations, there has to be unanimity. Hobbes fails to give any arguments in support of a simple majority, and he does not address the question of whether a sovereign state would be viable if only a slender majority voted it into being.

Second, when a civil society has already been established, it might well be an understood convention that dissenters accept the majority decision, even if they privately disagree with it (as in the concept of Cabinet collective responsibility). But the participants in this assembly are still in the state of nature, and they have no obligations at all until the social contract is agreed. They are certainly not contradicting themselves if they fail to accept the majority decision, because they are not party to it.

Third, the idea that there might be some people who did not participate in the assembly goes against my charitable interpretation of Hobbes as holding that the social contract was not a historical event. People could only fail to attend an event if that event actually occurred. But perhaps the non-participants could be interpreted as being people who are so unreflective about society and their relation to it that they have no sense of what they owe to society, and what society owes to them in return. Unfortunately there are many such people, and Hobbes's tough message is that they are effectively outlaws, and anyone can do to them what they please. However, this does not represent what Hobbes actually believed about the real world, because private citizens in a civil society cannot go around killing people just because they do not accept the social contract. In practice, Hobbes's position is that once a sovereign is in power, then they have the power to coerce people, whether they assented to the social contract or not.

iv. COMMONWEALTH BY INSTITUTION AND BY ACQUISITION

At the end of *Leviathan* chapter 17, Hobbes makes it explicit that a sovereign can gain power over people as much by force as through a social contract (CL 109–110):

> Absolute power can be obtained in two ways. One is by force, as when a father compels his sons to obey him, since he can take their lives away by depriving them of food; or as when someone allows conquered enemies to live, on condition that they do what he commands. The other way is when people voluntarily confer absolute power on one person or assembly in the hope of being protected. The latter is commonwealth by institution, the former is commonwealth by acquisition.

The theory of the social contract is an elegant way of making the concept of absolute power more palatable than it would otherwise be. People *ought* to positively want to live under an absolute sovereign, because life is better than under a divided authority or no authority at all. But, Hobbes's recognition that sovereignty can be gained by force of arms rather than through a contract is in danger of weakening his case. We have already seen that the drawing up of the contract cannot sensibly be understood as an actual historical event. But, what if *all* sovereigns originally gained power by force rather than by the democratic acclaim of the majority of citizens? This seems plausible, because where democracies have existed, they have generally emerged from more autocratic regimes. For example, the Athenian democracy, which was probably the purest form of democracy ever to have flourished in an advanced civilization, came after a long history of kings and tyrants. The lesson of history seems to be that democracy is a valuable prize, extracted from autocratic rulers after a long struggle, rather than that democracy is the natural condition in the state of nature, and that the democratic majority voluntarily renounce their authority to an absolute ruler.

If in fact commonwealths are all commonwealths by acquisition rather than by institution, this means that Hobbes's theory of the social contract makes sense only as a fiction which justifies our acquiescing in an absolute authority over us. As always, Hobbes's central point is that a single, absolute authority is better than a divided authority or no authority at all, and the theory of the social contract is a way of giving expression to this insight. It does not matter if the social contract never actually existed, because citizens can still recognize the advantages of living in a civil society, however it came into being.

Further evidence that actual power is more significant than the social contract is Hobbes's thesis that, if the sovereign loses the power to defend the citizens from war, then the contract is null and void, and the citizens have no further obligation. As he says in *Leviathan* chapter 21 (CL 144):

It is understood that the obligation which citizens have to the sovereign lasts as long as, but only as long as, the sovereign retains the power of protecting them. For the natural right of people to defend themselves when they cannot be protected by someone else cannot be extinguished by any contract. The sovereign is the soul of the state, and as soon as the soul is separated from the body, the parts of the body are no longer controlled by it.

This concession was politically important for Hobbes, because it enabled him to accept the authority of Cromwell's protectorate, despite his belief that the Civil War and the execution of Charles I were unjust.

At the beginning of *Leviathan* chapter 20, Hobbes says that the only difference between a commonwealth by institution and a commonwealth by acquisition is that in the first case people consent to it for fear of each other, whereas in the latter case they consent out of fear of the conqueror (CL 127):

> I call it a commonwealth by acquisition when sovereign power is acquired by force, so that, out of fear of death or prison, and whether individually or by majority vote, everyone binds themselves to do what it commands.
>
> And this kind of sovereignty or supreme power differs from that which comes into being by institution only in that the citizens accept rule over them in the latter case out of fear of each other, and in the former case out of fear of one person. However, in both cases they do it out of fear.

Since the powers of the sovereign are the same in each type of commonwealth, and it is now only a matter of history whether a commonwealth is by acquisition or by institution, the social contract should not be an essential element of Hobbes's political philosophy.

v. MONARCHY, ARISTOCRACY AND DEMOCRACY

As we have seen, Hobbes is generally careful to say that the sovereign is either an individual *or an assembly*. Depending on whether all the citizens or only a few of them constitute the assembly, we have three possible types of constitution: monarchy, aristocracy and democracy. As he says at the beginning of *Leviathan* chapter 19 CL 118):

> The difference between different types of commonwealth depends on the [legal] person holding absolute power. Absolute power must belong to one individual or many; and if many, it must either belong to everyone (so that everyone has the right to participate in the assembly), or it must belong to certain people who are distinguished from the rest. Consequently there are only three possible kinds of commonwealth. These are monarchy, where absolute power is vested in one individual; democracy, where absolute power is vested in an assembly which everyone is

entitled to attend; and aristocracy, where supreme power is vested in an assembly of citizens who are called nobles.

Although Hobbes was a royalist, it was politically convenient that he held both that sovereignty could be acquired by force, and that the sovereign could be an assembly. *Leviathan* was published just after Charles I had been executed, and the government taken over by the Parliamentarians (though Cromwell behaved increasingly like a monarch). However much Hobbes might have regarded the change of government as illegitimate, Parliament was the *de facto* sovereign, and it alone had the power to defend the life and well-being of the citizens it ruled over. This meant that Hobbes's political theory was potentially acceptable to both sides in the Civil War.

In chapter 19, Hobbes runs through some of the advantages and disadvantages of monarchy as opposed to rule by assembly. The first consideration is that monarchs owe their own prosperity to the prosperity of their people, whereas in democracy or aristocracy, people are more likely to enrich themselves through corruption or civil war (CL 120):

> The public good is maximized when public and private good are most inextricably united. But in a monarchy, public and private good are the same. For the wealth, power, and honour of the monarch depend on the strength and opinions of the citizens. This is because a monarch whose subjects are poor, weak, or wretched cannot be rich, or great, or secure. But in a democracy, the public good is often of less benefit to the private good of dishonest, greedy, or ambitious people than deceitful advice, treachery, or civil war.

Hobbes's argument may seem a strange one from a modern perspective, because we tend to hold that, if there is a sovereign at all, then their wealth should be kept entirely separate from the wealth of the nation. But, in Hobbes's day, when the sovereign's wealth was much more difficult to disentangle from that of the nation, there is a certainly plausibility to the view that the wealthier the nation, the wealthier the sovereign. We can also sympathize with his cynical attitude towards at least some politicians in a democracy. Nevertheless, history provides us with plenty of examples of nations where a fabulously rich sovereign presides over a citizenry living in grinding poverty, and of democracies with a far higher standard of living, despite widespread corruption.

The second consideration is that a monarch can obtain the advice of experts in secret, whereas the size of an assembly makes secrecy impossible. Moreover, assemblies do not allow non-members to speak, however expert, and their members are successful at acquiring wealth rather than knowledge. Hobbes may be right that democratic governments are bad at keeping confidential information, and rarely accept expert advice when it contradicts their policies; but, neither of these weaknesses is intrinsic to democracy as such, and they can be mitigated.

The third consideration is that, whereas monarchs change their minds no more than other human beings, decisions of assemblies depend on who happens to be present on any given occasion, and they can be changed from one day to the next. Although Hobbes does not give any concrete examples, he could have mentioned the way the Athenian assembly changed its mind on crucial decisions during the Peloponnesian War.

The fourth consideration is that monarchs cannot disagree with themselves out of envy or vested interest, whereas the members of an assembly can disagree with each other, even to the extent of causing a civil war. And since the only justification for its having sovereign power is to prevent civil war, this entirely defeats its purpose. Monarchy is the best guarantee of undivided sovereignty.

The fifth consideration is that monarchs can be persuaded by flatterers into enriching favourites and impoverishing enemies. But, Hobbes argues, there are limits to the number of favourites a monarch can have, and the number of favourites and relatives of the members of an assembly is much greater.

The sixth consideration is that the successor to a monarch is sometimes a child. But, Hobbes argues, this does not matter if the monarch made arrangements for a regent to act on the successor's behalf until the age of majority. And, he adds rather facetiously, assemblies are sometimes no better than a child, and themselves need a guardian or protector. Thus, in history there are many examples of a sovereign assembly appointing a dictator in times of great danger, such as war, as a kind of temporary monarch.

Hobbes's arguments for the superiority of monarchy over aristocracy or democracy are far from convincing. All the same, they are a clear expression of his preference for monarchy.

vi. THE INDIVISIBILITY OF SOVEREIGNTY

As we have just seen, one of the reasons why Hobbes prefers monarchy to aristocracy or democracy is because it is more likely to preserve the unity of sovereignty. In an assembly there are much more likely to be different factions, and as soon as one side refuses to accept a majority vote, there is a danger of civil war. Nevertheless, if there is just one assembly with ultimate authority over everything, sovereignty is still undivided unless it breaks down. But, to have a constitution which divides sovereignty between different individuals or bodies is a recipe for disaster, since any disagreement or conflict of interest cannot be resolved without the use of force. In *Leviathan* chapter 18, Hobbes attributes the recent Civil War to just this lack of agreement about a single authority (CL 117):

> In short, if any of the above powers [of the sovereign] are lacking, all the rest will disappear, and there will be a separation of powers about which Christ himself said 'A kingdom divided against itself cannot stand'. For unless there is first such a separation of powers, there will never be a separation of the people into opposed armies. The opinion of those who hold that the powers of the Kingdom of England are divided between the king, the Lords, and the House of Commons was the cause of the civil war which followed. The disputes about political and theological issues have even educated the people about the nature of sovereign power to such an extent that I believe there are now very few people in England who fail to see that the above powers are inseparable . . .

Political philosophers are divided as to whether or not there should be a separation of powers. The argument for separating them is to provide checks and balances which prevent a government from abusing its powers. The argument for undivided sovereignty is that separation of powers leads at best to indecision, and at worst to civil war. Since Hobbes's day, the British (unwritten) constitution has moved in the direction of the absolute sovereignty of the House of Commons, whereas the constitution of the United States has always been premised upon the separation of powers. In the subsequent three centuries, the United States has had one civil war, and the United Kingdom none; but it is not obvious that the difference has anything to do with the separation of powers. A modern Hobbesian would have to appeal to Yugoslavia, Somalia or Iraq in recent times as examples of countries where the removal of an absolute dictator led to civil war and the complete collapse of society. And an opponent of Hobbes might cite Zimbabwe as an example of a country where the failure to remove an absolute dictator has had exactly the same effect.

Although Hobbes uses a historical example in the above passage, his real reason for maintaining the indivisibility of sovereignty is logical and theoretical. As he says in *Leviathan* chapter 19 (CL 119):

> Therefore once a monarchy has been set up, no-one else can legally be chosen to represent the body of citizens, except that the monarch can explicitly choose someone to do so for a strictly defined purpose. For otherwise two or more persons would have absolute power in one and the same state, which would lead to a situation of war of all against all, which is contrary to the purpose of a commonwealth by institution.

vii. LIFE UNDER ABSOLUTE RULE

The popular view of life in a Hobbesian state is that it is pretty miserable, even if it is not 'solitary, poor, nasty, brutish, and short'. Hobbes himself is partly responsible for this impression, when he justifies absolute rule by saying that, however bad it is, it is not as bad as the state of nature. Thus, towards the end of *Leviathan* chapter 20, he says (CL 135):

But although people can imagine many evil consequences of unlimited power, the consequences of limited power are much worse, namely war of everyone against their neighbours. In this life, the human condition will never be without its downside.

In fact Hobbes was much more optimistic than this. In *Leviathan* chapter 18, he lists 13 powers or rights which the sovereign must retain in order not to lose absolute authority:

- the subjects cannot change the form of government;
- no one can be freed from subjection to the sovereign;
- anyone who dissented from the covenant must accept the majority decision;
- no one can complain about the sovereign's actions;
- the sovereign cannot be punished by the subjects;
- the sovereign must decide what is best for the peace and defence of the realm;
- the sovereign must decide which religious or political doctrines can be expressed in public;
- the sovereign must prescribe civil laws;
- the sovereign must control the judiciary;
- the sovereign must decide on peace and war, and be the generalissimo of the army;
- the sovereign must appoint holders of public offices;
- the sovereign is responsible for punishments and rewards;
- the sovereign must control the honours system.

We might well question how far it is necessary for all these powers to be in the hands of a single person or body in order to prevent the state from descending into civil war. We are now used to stable democracies (which Hobbes would actually classify as aristocracies) in which there is, for instance, a clear separation of powers between the legislature and the judiciary. Nevertheless, Hobbes's list of government functions is really quite minimalist, and it omits a wide range of areas which we would take for granted as state responsibilities: finance, taxation (which Hobbes mentions only in relation to war), trade, education, health, welfare and so on. But, these are areas which were not considered to be state functions in the seventeenth century.

So, if we consider the *scope* of government, Hobbes took it for granted that the sovereign, despite having absolute power, would not bother to exercise it over the everyday, private lives of citizens. They would have much more freedom from central control than we have become accustomed to in the modern world. If Hobbes could be brought to life again today, he would be far more horrified by the level of state control over minute details of our lives than we are shocked by his belief in the absolute power of the sovereign. As he says, rather optimistically, in *Leviathan* chapter 21, the sovereign cannot regulate everything, and citizens are free to do anything not explicitly prohibited (CL 138):

> These *artificial* chains [i.e. civil laws] are what I understand to be opposed to the freedom of citizens. For since it is impossible to regulate all actions by laws, it is said that a citizen has *freedom* with respect to all those actions about which the laws are silent, and with respect to those alone. In such matters, everyone is free to do what they think is in their best interest.

And in the English version, he is more specific about what the laws are silent about:

> ... the freedom to buy and sell, and otherwise make contracts with each other; to choose where to live, what to eat, what way of life to follow, how to bring up their children as they think fit; and so on.

As we now know, Hobbes was wrong about the extent to which it is possible to regulate citizens' behaviour by laws, because the massive increase in the size of the state and modern technology have made it possible for people's lives to be much more tightly controlled.

A further reason for the sovereign not to interfere in the private lives of citizens derives from the social contract. Hobbes says that the sovereign is not bound by the contract and therefore cannot break it, because the contract was made by the people with each other and not with the sovereign. Nevertheless, the contract and the laws of nature do provide a moral framework, limiting the activities of the sovereign to the purpose of the contract. Since the purpose of the contract was to protect people from civil war and external invasion, the powers of the sovereign should be limited to anything necessary to preserve peace – and this is the rationale for Hobbes's list of rights and powers above. As he says at the beginning of *Leviathan* chapter 30 (CL 219):

> The duties of the sovereign, whether a monarch or an assembly, are clearly indicated by the purpose for which sovereignty was established, namely *the safety of the people*. The sovereign is obliged by the law of nature to preserve their safety as far as possible, and is accountable to God, and to God alone. By 'the safety of the people' I mean not just the life of citizens, but also the comforts of life which individual citizens have justly acquired without harm or danger to the state.

The message is clear: that the sovereign should interfere with people's private lives only if they are a danger to the peace.

Now there is the question of whether an absolute ruler will make the lives of citizens worse than a ruler with limited powers, setting aside the question of whether or not a division of powers will inevitably lead to the disaster of civil war. Opinion is divided between those who hold that absolute power corrupts and that anyone in power must be restrained by checks and balances, and those who hold that checks and balances are largely ineffective, and whether power is exercised well or badly depends mainly on other factors. Hobbes belongs to the latter camp, and there is much to be said in support of his position.

We know from history, for example from the history of the Roman Empire that some emperors were very good and some were very bad. Under the good emperors, citizens could expect justice, security and prosperity. Under bad ones, they suffered arbitrary punishment and death, a breakdown of law and order, poor trading conditions, high taxation and external threats to security – quite apart from the moral depravation of the emperors' private lives.

However, all the emperors had the same absolute power, so the difference between good and bad emperors cannot be explained in terms of their power. Rather, it is to be explained in terms of their individual characters. Conversely, some states without a single sovereign authority are well run, whereas others are rife with corruption and injustice. So again the fact that power is divided between different individuals and bodies seems largely irrelevant, and the difference between well run and badly run states seems to depend more on history and culture than on the form of government.

We have already seen that Hobbes held that sovereigns have a strong motive to foster the prosperity and wellbeing of their people, because that will enhance their own wealth, honour and security. But another factor is that Hobbes takes it for granted that, at least in Europe and European colonies, the sovereign will be a committed Christian. Indeed, Part 3 of *Leviathan* (chapters 32–43) is entitled *Of a Christian Commonwealth*; and Hobbes assumes that, although sovereigns are as liable to human weaknesses as anyone else, they will run the state in accordance with Christian principles, at least as they interpret them. In short, although it is certainly possible for absolute rulers to become despotic, there is a good chance that they will rule wisely and well.

viii. FREEDOM OF THOUGHT

For someone living in a liberal democracy, perhaps the most disturbing item in Hobbes's list of sovereign powers is censorship of the written and spoken word. As he says in *Leviathan* chapter 18 (CL 113):

> Seventhly, it belongs to absolute power to decide what doctrines promote the preservation or violation of peace; and when, how far, and what doctrines are permitted in speeches before an audience; and what books are to be published, and who they are to be censored by. For opinions give rise to actions, therefore regulating citizens consists in regulating opinions, and this gives rise to peace and harmony. For true doctrines cannot be contrary to peace, any more than peace and harmony can be said to be

contrary to the laws of nature. In some states, through the negligence or ignorance of tutors and teachers, errors can gradually become universally accepted as true, and truths become offensive. . . . It therefore belongs to absolute power to judge all opinions and doctrines since they are very often the cause and origin of discord and civil war.

There are four things to note here. First, Hobbes sees it as a necessary truth that true political doctrines are conducive to peace, since they derive from the laws of nature, which are all about preserving peace. The corollary is that, if anyone promulgates the opposite, then they are promoting falsehoods which endanger the peace, and which therefore should be suppressed.

Second, in Hobbes's day, censorship of publications was standard practice in Europe, and his insistence that the sovereign had a duty to carry out censorship would not have been considered unusual or oppressive.

Third, Hobbes was writing during the Civil War, which was caused in large part by disagreements over religion and politics. Hobbes believed, with some plausibility that if King Charles I had had the power to suppress the views of puritans and anti-royalists, the Civil War would never have occurred. But the division of power between the king and parliament, the relative freedom of the universities to teach what they thought fit and a similar freedom of preaching in churches, meant that anti-royalist sentiments had a wide airing. With the benefit of hindsight, we might judge that the erosion of monarchical power that resulted from the execution of Charles and the subsequent puritan regime was ultimately a good thing; but from Hobbes's perspective, the horrors of the Civil War were an unmitigated disaster, and anything was preferable to allowing them to recur.

Fourth, Hobbes is only talking about what is said or written in the public domain, and on matters relevant to public security such as religion, politics and law. There is no question of attempting to control people's private thoughts: people can think what they like, provided that their public utterances are consistent with the law as decreed and interpreted by the sovereign. Nor is there any suggestion of censoring or spying on private gatherings of people or private correspondence. As long as people conform in public, they can say what they like in private.

But one kind of institution would be seriously affected by Hobbes's prohibition of public dissent, namely the universities. The large majority of people who wrote books or spoke in public on religion, politics or the law were graduates of England's two universities, Oxford and Cambridge. They were therefore largely responsible for formulating and publicizing the dissenting religious and political ideas which brought about the Civil War. Hobbes criticized the universities on a number of grounds.

First, at least until the time of Henry VIII, the universities owed their charter and loyalty not to the English sovereign, but to the Catholic Pope. It was a classic case of divided authority if the universities did not recognize the authority of the sovereign on religious matters, and Hobbes thoroughly approved of Henry's decision to declare himself and not the Pope to be head of the Church in England. It would be wrong to describe the universities as hotbeds of Catholicism by the time Hobbes wrote *Leviathan*, but they were far from slavish followers of the royal line on religious matters.

Second, by their very nature, universities encouraged debate and controversy. At the core of university teaching methods was the disputation, in which students had to defend or oppose controversial and sometimes quite paradoxical theses. This encouraged a spirit of freethinking which was fundamentally opposed to Hobbes's view that teachers and students should accept the doctrines of the head of the Church without question. The same was true of other areas of university teaching, in particular politics and the law, where students would entertain ideas quite inconsistent with the actual constitution and laws of England. In particular, they would study the works of Aristotle and other ancient authors, which generally favoured views of the state in which citizens did not hand over their rights to an absolute sovereign.

Third, universities encouraged the belief that their teachers and graduates were experts in their disciplines, and therefore that their opinions were superior to those of mere amateurs. Hobbes had a very low opinion of what was taught at universities. Mathematics was hardly studied at all (at least at the time when he was a student), and scientific knowledge had barely advanced since the time of Aristotle. The scientific ideas he himself published in *On Body* and other writings were far more solid and up-to-date than anything taught in the universities. In theology and law, academics were just wrong if they believed that such expertise as they had entitled them to say what was or was not true Christian belief, or what should be legal or not. These were matters for decision by the head of the Church and the sovereign of the civil state; and if there were any ambiguities in these decisions, they were to be resolved by the sovereign, and not by academics. As we have already seen, Hobbes believed he was the first to turn political theory into a science, and he therefore recommended that Leviathan be used as a university text book. As he writes in the 'Review and Conclusion' of the English version (CL 496):

> To conclude, there is nothing in this whole book, nor in what I previously wrote on the same subject in Latin, as far as I can see, which goes against either the word of God, or good behaviour; or tends to the disturbance of public peace. Therefore I think it advantageous for it to be printed, and more advantageous for it to be taught in the universities, provided those who judge it agree. For since the universities are the fountains of civil and moral doctrine, from which preachers and the gentry, drawing what water they find there, sprinkle it on the people (both from the pulpit and in conversation), great care should be taken that it is unpolluted by the poison of heathen political theorists, or by the spells of deceiving spirits.

Hobbes's fourth objection to universities (already mentioned in Chapter 2 section xii) is that academics speak and write in meaningless jargon, partly to cover their own ignorance, and partly to gain power and influence over others by impressing them with their apparent superior knowledge and understanding.

It is ironic that Hobbes, who was such an original and independent-minded thinker on political and theological issues, should advocate a complete ban on discussing them in public or at university.

CHAPTER 6

RELIGION

i. HOBBES AS A FUNDAMENTALIST ANGLICAN

Hobbes was a committed Anglican. As such, he was opposed both to Catholicism, which was still seen as a threat to religious and political stability, and to the Presbyterianism which the Scots were trying to impose on the English in return for their support of the Parliamentarians against King Charles I. The last part of *Leviathan*, Of the Kingdom of Darkness (as contrasted with the previous part, Of a Christian Commonwealth), is a sustained attack on both Catholicism and Presbyterianism, especially the former. The climax of this part, in chapter 47 (CL 486–487), is a comparison between the papacy and the kingdom of fairies, in which Hobbes displays his mordant wit to the full. He kills two birds with one stone by ridiculing both the superstitious belief in fairies, and Catholic beliefs which he holds are on the same level:

> From the time when the Bishop of Rome was held to be the Universal Bishop, the Roman Catholic hierarchy can, not inappropriately, be compared to the tales told in England by old wives, children, and peasants about fairies, that is, shadows or spectres and the wicked things they do in the night.
>
> For anyone who considers the origin of so great an ecclesiastical empire must surely think that the papacy is nothing other than the huge ghost of the former huge Roman empire, sitting crowned on its grave . . .

Fairies are spirits, and ecclesiastics call themselves spiritual men. Fairies inhabit dark and lonely places, and graves. Similarly, ecclesiastics walk in the obscurity of their doctrines, in monasteries, churches, and cemeteries . . .

Ecclesiastics are accustomed to taking away the use of natural reason from young men through spells blended from metaphysics and miracles, so that they will blindly obey their orders. So also in folk tales, fairies are said to snatch children out of their cradles, and replace them with fools prone to mischief.

The folk tales do not say what laboratories or workshops fairies use for concocting their spells. But the workshops of the ecclesiastics are the universities, which they established for themselves by their own authority.

Whenever fairies are displeased with someone, they are said to send one of their number to pinch them. Likewise, when the ecclesiastics are angry with some state or king, they send their superstitious and brainwashed subjects to pinch them by sedition, or sometimes even make kings pinch each other . . .

Fairies have no existence except in the fear and imagination of ignorant people. Similarly, the spiritual power of the Pope (apart from his own secular rule) consists only in the fear of excommunication.

When I describe Hobbes as a fundamentalist Anglican, I mean that he believed in the absolute authority of the Bible and the Book of Common Prayer – and nothing else. And if there is any inconsistency between the two, the Bible must come first, even though Hobbes accepts that, since the Book of Common Prayer carries the authority of the sovereign, he must not publicly disagree with it. Thus, in chapter 1 of the Appendix to the Latin *Leviathan*, which takes the form of a dialogue between A and B, Hobbes writes (CL 519):

A. So the next question to be asked is whether expressions such as 'incorporeal substance', 'immaterial substance', or 'separate essences' are found in Holy Scripture.

B. These expressions are not in Holy Scripture. But the first of the 39 Articles of Religion, published by the Anglican Church in 1562, explicitly states that 'God is without a body and without parts.' Therefore it is not to be denied. Besides, it has been decreed that the punishment for denying it is excommunication.

A. It will not be denied. However, in the 20th Article it is said that the Church should not tell anyone to believe anything which cannot be deduced from Holy Scripture. If only it had been so deduced!

Hobbes could hardly make it clearer that he personally believes that the first of the 39 Articles is wrong.

Wherever possible, Hobbes supports his philosophical claims with references to the Bible, and, as we have already seen in the case of the immaterial soul, he uses the absence of a doctrine in the Bible as an argument for not believing in it. It is ironical that Hobbes's enemies often called him an atheist because of his materialism, when his writings (especially *Leviathan*) include far more scriptural references than those of other philosophers. There can be no doubt about the sincerity of his Christian belief. When his sincerity was questioned, he gave as evidence that he had summoned an Anglican priest to deliver the last rites when he was so ill in Paris that he thought he was going to die.

Although he regarded the Bible as the ultimate authority on religious matters, he did not believe that it had to be taken literally. This meant that there was scope for different interpretations. And if there are different interpretations of a book as crucially important as the Bible, people are unlikely to be able to persuade others, merely by the use of reason, that their interpretation is better. The result could be religious civil war. So, just as the sovereign was the sole authority on civil matters, similarly the sovereign was the sole authority on religious matters, and in particular on the interpretation of the Bible. The sovereign was both head of state and head of the Anglican church, thus making England a kind of theocracy, or Christian Commonwealth.

The most powerful argument against the right of the sovereign to interpret the Bible would be that a private citizen had been directly inspired by God with a different interpretation. Hobbes rejects this possibility on the grounds that direct inspiration would be a miracle, and the age of miracles had come to an end. As he says in *Leviathan* chapter 32 (CL 249):

> Since the age of miracles has ceased, we have no criterion for recognising the revelation or inspiration of any private person, nor have we any obligation to accept what they say. We have nothing other than the holy scriptures, which have taken the place of miracles since the time of the apostles, and are a sufficient compensation for the end of prophecy. Through correct interpretation and careful reasoning from these scriptures, it is easy to deduce the precepts and rules that are necessary for knowing our duties both towards God and towards our fellow human beings, without enthusiasm, or divine inspiration.

We have already seen that Hobbes included the interpretation of the Bible among the powers of the sovereign. In *Leviathan* chapter 40 (CL 321), he compares this power with the authority of Moses as the sole mediator between God and humankind, and the only person allowed to climb Mount Sinai, where Moses received the ten commandments:

> ... the person who, in a Christian commonwealth, has the same position as Moses is the sole messenger of God, and the sole interpreter of his commands; and in the interpretation of holy scripture, no-one has the right to cross the limits set by the sovereign. For the holy scriptures, through which God speaks to us today, are like Mount Sinai, in which the limits set are the laws of those who represent God's person on earth. It is permitted to look upon these laws, and to learn from them to fear God. But it is to overstep the limits set by God if we interpret them, that is, if we inquisitively pry into what God has said to those whom he has made our rulers, and make ourselves the judges of whether they rule us in the way God has commanded them.

This seems to conflict with what Hobbes said earlier about the social contract, namely that the sovereign receives authority from the people, and can arbitrarily decide how the Bible is to be interpreted by virtue of their absolute power. Here he says that the sovereign was appointed by God, and that God tells the sovereign how the Bible is to be interpreted. However, the two positions can be reconciled if we bear in mind that, for Hobbes, God is ultimately responsible for everything that happens in the universe. Both the decision of the people to appoint that particular sovereign, and the way the sovereign interprets the Bible, are outcomes of the divine act of creation.

ii. THE CORRUPTION OF CHRISTIANITY BY GREEK PHILOSOPHY

By accepting only the Bible as an authority on religious matters, Hobbes was committed to rejecting any religious doctrines thought up after the Bible was written. In practice this meant everything after the publication of the Nicene Creed, which Hobbes held to be the last official pronouncement that adhered strictly to the Bible. This creed was the outcome of the Council of Nicaea (the modern İznik, in Turkey), convened by the Emperor Constantine in AD 325 to combat the Arian heresy, according to which Jesus the son was not of the same substance as God the father. Hobbes devotes the first chapter of the Appendix to the Latin *Leviathan* to interpreting the Nicene Creed.

However, Hobbes did not merely ignore post-Biblical theology: he produced an ingenious and thoroughly original argument for rejecting it as not merely false, but meaningless. In *Leviathan* chapter 46 ('The darkness from vacuous philosophy'), he starts by distinguishing genuine philosophy, such as his own, from the corrupt philosophy of the Aristotelians in particular (CL 468–469):

> Reader, you will be disappointed if you are expecting this chapter to be a diatribe against philosophy or philosophers. What will it be, then? I distinguish between philosophers and non-philosophers, and between true and false philosophy. The former is the wisest teacher of how human life should be lived, and the

crowning glory of human nature. The latter, which has for long been considered the true philosophy, is a painted and garrulous whore. For philosophy is the search after wisdom; and in so far as it is true philosophy, it is wisdom. It can be defined as: scientific knowledge, acquired by correct reasoning, of effects from their conceived causes or origins, and of possible origins from known effects. This wisdom is neither prohibited by Scripture, nor rejected by any human being.

As we have already seen, Hobbes effectively equates genuine philosophy with science, and rejects a metaphysics which deals merely in abstractions. It is only the latter that brings about darkness through its vacuity.

He then provides a brief historical sketch of how the early church was hijacked by Aristotelian philosophers who converted to Christianity, but without abandoning their philosophical pretensions. Later, with the foundation of the universities from the eleventh century onwards in the West, Aristotle was regarded as 'the one great father of the Church', and his philosophy was taught and preached as integral to Catholic theology. But Aristotle's philosophy was based on a fundamental mistake, which was responsible for all the erroneous, non-Biblical doctrines of the Catholic church. Hobbes writes (CL 473–474):

It might be said: 'You attack Roman Catholic doctrine, or the theology taught in the universities, on the grounds that it is Aristotelian. But how is it derived from Aristotle, and from what Aristotelian opinions?' I shall tell you. When the Greeks, the Latins, and most Europeans affirm something, they combine two names with the word 'to be'. This is how they indicate that both names are names of one and the same thing. For example, someone who says 'A human is an animal,' wants to be understood as if they had said 'If we are correct in saying that some particular thing is a human, we are also correct in saying that the same thing is an animal.' On other occasions, they attach the word 'to be' to a single name, as when someone says 'God is.' But in this case, they want to be understood as if they had said

'God is something real, not a figment of the mind – a *hypostasis* [the Greek for "substance"], not a phantasm.' This is how the Greeks distinguished between genuine things, and things which are only apparent. For example, they called a person looking at themselves in a mirror a *hypostasis* or 'substance'; but they called their image seen in the mirror a 'phantasm'. When the word 'to be' is taken in the first way, namely when it combines two names, it is called the 'copula'; and when it is taken in the other way, it is called the 'substantive verb'. Even the Hebrews used the substantive verb from time to time, as when God says without qualification that his name is 'I am'; but they never used the word 'to be' as a copula. Instead of using the copula, the Hebrews put two names in apposition. For example, Genesis 1.2 has 'Earth thing without form,' whereas we necessarily have to translate it as 'The Earth was without form.'

Hobbes's point is that, in languages related to Greek and Latin, the verb 'to be' has two functions. One is to indicate that the subject of the sentence actually exists as a substance in its own right – and this is a function shared with Hebrew, in which it possible to say that God and other beings exist. (He overlooks the fact that in languages such as English, we distinguish between 'is' and 'exists'. In English, we do not say, as was said in Latin, that 'Troy was', to mean that Troy no longer existed, or in Italian, that 'Othello was', to mean that Othello was about to be 'history' – but this does not affect Hobbes's argument.) The other function of the verb 'to be' is to join two names together so that one (the predicate) is attributed to the other (the subject). As in Hobbes's example, being an animal (predicate) is attributed to a human (the subject). But, the only words to have any meaning are 'human' and 'animal'. The verb 'to be' does not add anything, and its sole function is grammatical, rather like a punctuation mark. There are languages, such as Hebrew, which convey precisely the same meaning as the English simply by putting the names side-by-side, and without using the verb 'to be'. And even in English, there can be snappy slogans which leave it out, such as 'Two wheels good'.

Having established that the verb 'to be' is redundant, Hobbes continues:

> Aristotle was more interested in words than in things. He understood what things were to be understood by the names 'human' and 'animal', for example. But not content with that, this diligent man went further, and asked what sort of thing was to be conceived through the copula 'is', or at least through the infinitive 'to be'. He never doubted that the name 'to be' was the name of some *thing*, as if there were something in the real world of which the name was 'being' or 'essence.' From this absurdity he fell into an even worse one, namely he asserted that some of these essences could become separated from the individual beings they belonged to, occupy the celestial spheres, and drive them round. He also held that the human soul could be separated and removed from the human being, and continue to exist on its own – a doctrine which might perhaps be consistent with Homer's theology, but not with Holy Scripture. The word 'essence' is not to be found in Scripture, nor in the liturgy, articles, or canons of the Anglican Church. Nor is the Greek word *ousia* ['being'], except in the sense of 'riches' (the Latin *res* also carries both these senses). Nor again 'essential', 'essentiality', 'entity', or 'entitative', or any word formed from the copula. Hebrew did not have this problem. So an essence is not a thing, whether created or uncreated, but an artificially made up name. Entangled by words, whether written or spoken, Aristotle by himself gave birth to such novel, bastard, and empty beings by means of the copulation of names, and they are the original sources of the philosophy which St Paul calls an 'empty deceit.'

This passage is a brilliant use of linguistic analysis to demolish a vast edifice of metaphysical doctrine – a single brick is removed, and everything collapses. Hobbes's central point is that Aristotle made the mistake of assuming that words can be meaningful only if there is something corresponding to them in reality. In fact there is nothing corresponding to the verb 'to be', because its sole function is to make a grammatical connection between the subject and the predicate. But Aristotle believed that, in addition to the material objects denoted by names such as 'human' and 'animal', there must also exist immaterial 'beings' or 'essences' (which is just a Latin word for 'beings') corresponding to the verb 'to be'. He treated these beings as existing in their own right, and explained the motions of the heavenly bodies as due to invisible beings pushing them round in their circular motions, and explained the behaviour of the human body as due to an immaterial soul which could survive the destruction of the body. Hobbes held that all the meaningless beliefs in immaterial beings and abstract entities which characterized scholastic philosophy and Catholic theology had their ultimate source in Aristotle's assumption that there must be some immaterial entity corresponding to the verb 'to be'. Hobbes is almost certainly going too far in claiming that this one word is alone responsible for the whole of meaningless metaphysics; but his insight that metaphysics is parasitic on accidental features of particular languages is one that remained largely forgotten until it was rediscovered by philosophers such as Wittgenstein in the twentieth century.

To return to Hobbes's fundamentalism, he emphasizes that the Old Testament, which was written in Hebrew, has no taint of the immaterialism of later Greek philosophy. One might expect the New Testament to be different, because it was written in Greek, and some of its authors (especially St John of the gospel) were clearly aware of and influenced by Greek philosophical ideas. Nevertheless, Hobbes does seem to be correct that the immaterialism he especially objects to is not present in the New Testament either. The malign influence of Greek philosophy made its presence felt only when theologians started relying on their own philosophical reasoning in order to establish religious truths, instead of limiting themselves to the authority of the Bible. It reached its peak when St Thomas Aquinas (1225–1274) incorporated Aristotelian philosophy into Christian theology, and the Catholic church recognized this new theology as official. From then onwards, Catholic theology and university philosophy degenerated into the meaningless jargon and abstract terms Hobbes repeatedly makes fun of. For example, at the end of the English version of *Leviathan* chapter 8 (CL 46–47), Hobbes says:

And in particular, on the question of transubstantiation, where after certain words spoken [by the priest in mass], those who say that the white*ness*, round*ness*, magni*tude*, quali*ty*, corruptibili*ty*, all of which are immaterial, etc. go out of the wafer into the body of our blessed Saviour, do they not make those *nesses, tudes*, and *ties*, to be so many spirits possessing his body? For by spirits they always mean things which, despite being immaterial, are nevertheless movable from one place to another. So this kind of absurdity can rightly be included as one of the many sorts of madness.

Hobbes's point is that only material objects can move in space and time, and that it is absurd to suppose that qualities of the wafer can be transferred to the body of Christ. Catholic theology was ultimately corrupted by Aristotle's mistaken belief that *nesses, tudes* and *ties* could be derived from a fictitious concept of *being*, corresponding to the meaningless copula 'to be'.

Finally, we should note Hobbes's clever pun, when he says that by the copulation of names, Aristotle gave birth to ridiculous and empty beings.

iii. THE ARGUMENT FOR BELIEF IN THE EXISTENCE OF GOD

In proving the existence of God, Hobbes was faced with the problem that the only evidence he accepts is either the evidence of the senses, or a proof based on reasoning. Obviously the Christian God is not the sort of being whose existence can be proved by experience – unlike pagan gods, which were believed to inhabit the earth (for example, on the summit of Mount Olympus), and to interact with humans from time to time. So, his existence would have to be proved by reason. However, as we saw in Chapter 2, reasoning depends on definitions, and we can only have absolute certainty when we define things we know how to create, such as geometrical figures. And obviously again, God is not something we create, but it is God who creates us.

Moreover, the problem is not simply one of proof, but of whether we can have any conception of God at all. Hobbes held that all our conceptions are derived from experience, and that, since we do not have an experience of God, we cannot have any conception of him. So even if we do manage to prove the existence of God, how can we know what have we proved the existence of, given that we have no conception of him?

Hobbes was quite adamant that we have no conception of God. This is central to his rejection of one of Descartes' arguments for the existence of God in *Meditation* III. Descartes claimed that his mind contained an idea of God: 'supreme, eternal, infinite, omniscient, omnipotent, and creator of everything that exists, apart from himself'. He then argued that this idea was so much greater than Descartes himself that he could not possibly have thought it up from his own resources, as he could the idea of a chimaera, for example. Consequently the idea must have come from God himself, thus proving that he exists.

Hobbes's response was simply to deny that we have any idea of God at all. In the fifth *Objection*, he says:

> . . . we have no image or idea corresponding to the holy name of God. This is why we are forbidden to worship God through images, in case we come to think we can form a conception of him who cannot be conceived. So it seems we have no idea of God within ourselves.

But, if we can have no conception of God, what do our words mean when we use language to describe him? Hobbes answers this question in the *Elements of Law* chapter 11 section 3:

> Admittedly we attribute things like seeing, hearing, speaking, knowing, and loving to God Almighty. When we attribute these names to *people*, we have an understanding of something which is in those people; but when we attribute them to God, they give us no understanding of anything in his nature. It is a good argument that God who made the eye should be able to see; and that God who made the ear should be able to hear. But it is an equally good argument to say that God who made the eye should be able to see without the eye; or that God who made the ear

should be able to hear without the ear; or that God who made the brain should be able to know without having a brain; or that God who made the heart should be able to love without having a heart. Therefore the attributes which are applied to the Deity are such as to signify either our incapacity or our reverence: our incapacity when we say he is incomprehensible and infinite; and our reverence when we give him the names which, amongst ourselves, are the names of the things we most praise and commend, for example, 'omnipotent', 'omniscient', 'just', 'merciful', etc. And when God Almighty gives these names to himself in the Scriptures, it is merely *anthropomorphically*, that is to say, by descending to our way of speaking, otherwise we would be incapable of understanding him.

This answer is a highly sophisticated one. Hobbes demonstrates that he has advanced well beyond a primitive linguistics in which it is assumed that the primary function of language is to describe. In the case of religious language, the adjectives we apply to God do not constitute a description at all, and we do not have any concept of God in our minds consisting of the totality of those adjectives – or if we do have any mental picture in our minds, it is as misleading as imagining God to be an old man with a grey beard sitting on a cloud. Rather, they are what came to be known as 'performative utterances' in the twentieth century (a term coined by J. L. Austin). In other words, their function is not to make true or false claims about the nature of reality, but to have a ritual significance. By applying these adjectives to God, we acknowledge our distance from him which means that we cannot comprehend his nature at all, and at the same time worship him. And to worship God is a totally different activity from describing him. But what grounds does Hobbes have for believing in the existence of God at all?

Unlike earlier philosophers, such as Aquinas and Descartes, who gave a range of arguments for the existence of God, Hobbes wisely stuck to one. It was wise of him, because if an argument is valid, there is no need for additional arguments. Giving more than one argument implies that none of them is sufficient by itself, and that God's existence can only be established by the accumulation of circumstantial evidence. Hobbes's argument first occurs in the *Elements of Law* chapter 11 section 2, and he repeats it in much the same form in later writings:

> Since God Almighty is incomprehensible, it follows that we can have no conception or image of the Deity. Consequently, all his attributes signify our inability and lack of power to conceive anything about his nature. They give us no conception of him, except *that there is a God*. For the effects which it is our nature to believe in necessarily include a power of creating them before they were created; and that power presupposes something existent which has such a power; and if the existent thing which has such a creative power were not eternal, it must necessarily have been created by something before it; and that again by something else before it – until we come to an eternal power, that is to say, to the first power of all powers, and first cause of all causes. And this is what all people call by the name 'God', implying eternity, incomprehensibility, and omnipotence. In this way, anyone who thinks about the matter can know by nature *that* God exists, though not *what* he is – just as someone who is born blind cannot have any imagination of what kind of thing fire is, but they cannot fail to know that there is something which people call 'fire', because it warms them.

Again, Hobbes's argument is quite sophisticated. He avoids the logical trap of what is known as the 'first cause argument', which runs roughly as follows:

> Every event has a cause;
> If the chain of causes and effects goes back to infinity, there is nothing to cause it to begin;
> Therefore there must be a first, uncaused cause.

This argument is blatantly illogical, because the conclusion contradicts the first premise. You cannot derive from the premise that every event has a cause the conclusion that there is one event that has no cause. Instead, Hobbes gives what was later called the 'cosmological argument', which is the following:

Every event in the natural world has a cause;
If the chain of causes and effects goes back to infinity, there is nothing to cause it to begin;
Therefore there must be a supernatural, eternal cause, separate from the chain of causes and effects in the natural world.

This argument is better, because it is logically consistent, and it points to a creator God distinct from the chain of natural events (he is of a different order of being from, say, the big bang). Nevertheless, it is still less than conclusive, because it is only an unproved assumption that every event has a cause, and it is logically invalid to argue from what we do know, to an entirely different order of reality of which we have no knowledge at all. Given Hobbes's insistence that we can know only what is given in experience and what is deducible from it by reason, he has no right to say that God's existence can be proved. As a protestant, he might have been better off arguing that justification is by faith alone, rather than by reason. And as a Hobbesian, he might have been better off arguing that, as a citizen of a Christian Commonwealth, belief in God (or at least a declared belief in God) was a requirement under the social contract. However, although Hobbes's argument for the existence of God is flawed, there can be no doubt of the sincerity of his belief.

Hobbes's analogy of a blind person in front of a fire deserves some comment. He explains it more fully in his fifth Objection to Descartes' *Meditations*:

So it seems we have no idea of God within ourselves. Rather we are like people who are born blind, but having on a number of occasions come near fires and felt their warmth, they recognise the existence of something causing the warmth; and hearing it called 'fire', they conclude that fire exists. However, they do not know what shape or colour fire has – in other words, they have before their minds absolutely no idea or image of fire. So if people know that there must be some cause of their images or ideas, and that there must be some other previous cause of the cause, and so on for ever, they are eventually forced to call a halt, by assuming some eternal cause, which cannot have any cause earlier than itself, since it never had a beginning to its existence. So they conclude that necessarily something eternal exists. However, they have no idea which they can call the idea of that eternal being, but they give a name to the thing they believe in or accept, and call it God.

At one level, what Hobbes says is preposterous. It is certainly true that a blind person has a less rich idea of fire than a sighted person. But, it is absurd to say that a blind person has no idea *at all* of fire, because they have direct experience of its most important feature, namely its warmth. A sighted person who had seen fires, but never been close enough to experience their warmth, would have an even more impoverished idea of fire. This is one of the rare instances where Hobbes seems to be thinking entirely in terms of vision, and neglecting the other senses.

However, at another level, Hobbes could be trying to make the better point that, since we know only the sensory images we have of external objects, and since we have good grounds for supposing that the qualities of things in themselves are quite unlike the qualities of sensory images, we can have no idea what external objects are like in themselves. Nevertheless, we are compelled to believe that external objects exist as the causes of our images, even though we have no idea of their real nature. Similarly, we are compelled to believe in God as the ultimate uncaused cause, even though we have absolutely no idea of his nature.

iv. GOD AS MATERIAL

In his earlier writings, Hobbes stresses that we can have no idea of God at all, except as the unknowable, eternal creator of the universe. However, in his later writings, he claims that one thing we can know about God is that he is material. This raises the question of whether he concealed his true belief when he was younger, or whether he changed his mind.

There is good reason for supposing that, if he believed that God was material, he would have kept quiet about it. As it happens, there were early religious authorities, of which Hobbes was well aware, for the belief that only material objects exist. In pre-Christian Judaism, the Sadducees held that God and human souls were material, and one of the earliest Christian fathers, Tertullian (c. 160–220) stated quite explicitly that God was material. Nevertheless, in the seventeenth-century England, 'sadducism', or the doctrine that there are no immaterial beings, was generally regarded as tantamount to atheism. In the context of Anglicanism, it was certainly contrary to the 39 Articles, promulgated in 1562, which begin 'There is but one living and true God, everlasting, without body, parts, or passions . . .'. As I said in Chapter 1, Hobbes was the subject of a House of Commons enquiry, and he destroyed many of his unpublished papers on theology in case they could be used against him. These would no doubt have provided us with much more information about Hobbes's religious beliefs than is obtainable from his published writings, and his destroying them implies that they were incriminating. He was only publicly explicit about God's materiality in writings printed abroad in Latin, and when he was in his eighties, and too old to be worth prosecuting. So, it is quite likely that Hobbes always believed God was material, but kept quiet about it when he was younger.

His most explicit statement is in the Appendix to *Leviathan*, chapter 3 (CL 540):

A. Then, near the beginning of the fourth chapter, he denies that there are any incorporeal substances. What else is this than to deny the existence of God, or to assert that God is body?

B. He does indeed assert that God is body. But Tertullian made the same assertion before him. Arguing against Apelles and other heretics of his time, who taught that our Saviour Jesus Christ was not a body but a phantasm, he made this general pronouncement that 'whatever is not a body is not a being.' Similarly against Praxeas: 'Every substance is a body of one kind or other.' This doctrine was not condemned in any of the first four general Councils. Show me, if you can, the words 'incorporeal' or 'immaterial' in the Scriptures.

Hobbes makes it clear that the materiality of God follows from his general thesis that 'body' and 'substance' have the same meaning, so that the expression 'immaterial substance' is a contradiction in terms. It is arguable that this is just about consistent with Hobbes's claim that we have no idea of God, since it is incomprehensible to us how an infinite material object can be the creator of the universe, and we can have no mental picture of such a being. Nevertheless, it is saying something more positive about God's nature than we find in Hobbes's earlier writings.

In the Latin, Hobbes's statement is almost shockingly stark: *Deus est corpus*. But it is ambiguous. Latin does not have a definite or an indefinite article, and the statement can be translated either as 'God is *a* body' or as 'God is *body*'. I prefer the latter, because 'God is a body' suggests that God is just one of many bodies, which would certainly be inconsistent with his infinite divinity. The statement is shocking because Hobbes does not use an adjective, such as 'corporeal' or 'material', but instead he *equates* God with body.

This gives rise to another problem of interpretation. If God is body and is infinite, the most natural interpretation is that God is identical with the whole of the infinite, material universe. The alternative is to say that, despite his wording, Hobbes does not mean to *equate* God with body, but merely to say that he is material, but distinct from the physical objects which constitute the observable universe. On this interpretation, he would have to be an infinite, all-pervasive material spirit – that is, a highly rarefied kind of matter, like the ether which carries light even where there is no air.

As Hobbes says in *An Answer to Dr. Bramhall* (p. 340):

From what I say about the universe, he [Dr. Bramhall] infers that I make God to be nothing. But his inference is absurd. What he could have inferred correctly is that I make God a corporeal, but pure spirit. By 'the universe,' I mean the aggregate of all things which have being in themselves; and that is what everybody else means too. And because God has a being, it follows that he is either the whole universe, or part of it.

This is a very clear statement that God is either the whole world or part of it; and when Hobbes says that God might be *part* of it, he must mean that he is part of it in the sense of being an all-pervasive material spirit filling all the spaces where there are no solid bodies. He tends towards the first position in his Latin writings printed abroad, and towards the second in his English writings published in England, perhaps because it would seem less heretical to the censors.

The first position would make Hobbes a pantheist, or someone who equates God with the whole of nature. If so, he would be neither the first nor the last pantheist. In antiquity the Stoic philosophers were pantheists, and, as we shall see in the next chapter, one of the philosophers most influenced by Hobbes, namely Spinoza (1632 1677), was also an avowed pantheist, who used the terms 'God' and 'nature' interchangeably. In this context, it is far from incredible that Hobbes should have literally equated God with body, and there are a number of passages in his Latin writings which support this interpretation. In the Appendix to *Leviathan* chapter 3, Hobbes writes (CL 541):

Again, 'We all have our being and move in God' – these are the words of Paul the Apostle in *Acts* 17.28. But we all have quantitative features, and can something which is quantitative have its being in something which is non-quantitative? God is great; but it is impossible to understand his greatness without body. Not even at the Council of Nicaea was it decreed that God is incorporeal.

Hobbes makes two points here. First there is the Biblical argument that, according to Paul, we are all *in* God; but since we have spatial dimensions, we can only exist in a being which also has spatial dimensions. Since having spatial dimensions is the defining characteristic of body, it follows that God is body, and that we are parts of the divine whole.

The second point is that God is great, and only a body can be great. Now this is true if 'great' means 'large'. But Hobbes knew perfectly well that the Latin words *magnus* and the superlative *maximus*, as well as meaning 'large' and 'largest', were honorific titles with no implications of physical size. As it happens, Charlemagne, or Charles the Great, was exceptionally tall; but he was called 'the Great' because of his exploits, and not because of his height. Similarly, God was called 'great' because of his power and status, and not because of his physical size. Hobbes's argument is simply invalid.

A little later in the same chapter, Hobbes writes as follows (CL 541):

> Besides, it was the intention of the Fathers at the Council of Nicaea to condemn not only Arianism, but all the heresies which had crept into the Church after the death of our Lord. One of these was the heresy of the anthropomorphites, who attributed the parts of the human body to God. But they did not condemn those who had written (along with Tertullian) that genuine, 'thingly', and pure spirit is corporeal. Those who attribute purity to God are right to do so, since it is an honorific title. But it is dangerous to describe him as a rarefied being, since rarefaction is on a scale leading to nothingness.

Here Hobbes seems to say that God is a spirit consisting of highly rarefied matter; but then he retracts on the grounds that the more rarefied matter becomes, the closer it comes to nothingness. So, a maximally rarefied spirit would be nothing at all. The implication is that solid matter is greater than spirit, because it is denser, and has more reality to it, so that God must be the totality of solid matter.

In his English writings, Hobbes leans towards the opposite view, that God is a material spirit filling the spaces between solid bodies. Indeed, in the English *Leviathan* chapter 31, he explicitly denies that God can be equated with the whole world (CL 239):

> ... those philosophers who said that the world, or the soul of the world, was God spoke unworthily of him, and denied his

existence. For by God is understood the cause of the world, and
to say that the world is God is to say that there is no cause of it,
in other words, no God.

But it is significant that Hobbes completely omitted this passage
from the Latin *Leviathan*, which implies either that he changed his
mind later, or that he felt it necessary to disguise his pantheistic
tendencies in a book for an English readership.

In *Ten Dialogues of Natural Philosophy* (p. 89), he writes:

> A. It is difficult to take as an assumption, and even more dif-
> ficult to believe, that the infinite and omnipotent Creator of all
> things should have produced something as vast as the world we
> see, without leaving a few little spaces with nothing at all in
> them. Relative to the universe as a whole, they would be
> insignificant.
>
> B. Why do you say that? Do you think it provides any argument
> to prove there is a vacuum?
>
> A. Why not? Given the rapid vibration of all natural bodies, why
> should not some small parts of them be thrown off, and leave
> empty the places they were thrown out of?
>
> B. Because he who created them is not a phantasm, but the most
> real substance that exists. Since he is infinite, no place where he is
> can be empty, and no place where he is not can be full . . .

Here Hobbes could hardly be clearer that God is a universal, material spirit. But how is this possible, given that he already holds that
there is no such thing as empty space, since the universe is filled with
an ether that transmits light? It is axiomatic that two bodies cannot
occupy the same space, so, if God is corporeal, he cannot occupy
the same space as the ether, and there is no room for him at all.
Consequently, he must *be* the ether. Hobbes never actually says
this, but there is an intriguing passage in *An Answer to Dr. Bramhall*
(pp. 309–10):

I, and many others, have seen an experiment with two types of water: river water, and a mineral water. Although they were indistinguishable from each other by sight, yet when they were mixed together, the compound substance was not visibly distinguishable from milk. However, we know that they were not blended in such a way that every part of the one was in every part of the other, since it is impossible for two bodies to be in the same place. The only way in which every part could be changed is by the *activity* of the mineral water, making the water appear differently to the senses, but without being everywhere and in every part of it. So if gross bodies such as these can have so much active power, what should we think of spirits, of which there are as many kinds as there are kinds of liquids, and which have greater active power? Can it then be doubted that God, who is an infinitely fine spirit, and intelligent too, can create and alter all species and kinds of body as he pleases? I dare not say that this is actually the way in which God operates, since it is beyond my comprehension. On the other hand, it is very useful for demonstrating that the omnipotence of God implies no contradiction; and it is better than reducing the Divine substance to a ghost or phantasm (i.e. *nothing*) through claiming to increase its fineness.

So, if God and the ether both existed, they would retain their separate identities, and God could only exist where the ether was not. This would severely restrict God's infinity. It is bad enough that, if he is a spirit and not the whole universe, he can exist only where there is no solid matter. But if he is jostling for space with the ether, there is very little room for a material God at all. If pressed, Hobbes would have to say that God *was* the all-pervasive ether.

v. THE AFTERLIFE

A central tenet of Christianity is that there is life after death, and that the virtuous will be rewarded and the wicked punished. However, there are different philosophical theories about how, when, and where. I shall consider the three most important approaches.

Perhaps the commonest belief today is that there is an immaterial soul which can exist separately from the body, and which goes straight to heaven or hell on the death of the body. It is left obscure where heaven and hell are (if it is even meaningful to give them a location), or how a disembodied soul can either enjoy pleasure or suffer pain. Clearly a disembodied soul cannot literally be burned to eternity in the fires of hell. The belief in an immaterial soul that is entirely independent of the body derives ultimately from Plato, and it was imported into Christianity first by St Augustine (354–430), and then again by Descartes in modern times.

However, the Platonic/Cartesian approach is very different from the official Catholic position dating back to Thomas Aquinas's amalgamation of Christian theology with Aristotelian philosophy in the middle ages. According to Aquinas, the soul is the form of the body, and it cannot exist without a body. On death, the soul cannot go straight to heaven or hell, but has to wait in limbo until the last judgment, when it is given a spiritual body to inform. It will then go to heaven or hell (wherever they are), and its spiritual body (whatever that is), will enable it to enjoy pleasure or suffer pain to eternity.

Hobbes would have none of this, because both the Platonic theory of the immaterial soul and the Aristotelian theory of the soul as the form of the body were imported from Greek philosophy, and were alien to the third theory, which is that of the Bible and the early Christians.

Hobbes maintained, with good Biblical and historical authority, that the early Christians believed that there was no immaterial soul, but that *bodies* would be resurrected at the last judgment, and that eternal life would be on earth. Concrete evidence for this (not mentioned by Hobbes) is that, whereas the pagan Greeks buried the dead in direct contact with the earth, so that the soul could be released from the body and travel to Hades, the early Christians buried the dead in sarcophagi and catacombs, so that the matter of the body would be kept free of contamination or dissipation, and thus be ready to be brought alive again at the second coming.

Hobbes was obviously committed to this position because of his denial of an immaterial soul; but he also cited Biblical evidence in support. Thus, in the Appendix to *Leviathan*, chapter 3, he says (CL 540):

> On my reading (*Matthew* 27.52), when Christ was dying on the cross, dead bodies were raised from the grave, not souls.

It was important for Hobbes that humans were not naturally immortal (as Descartes held), but that a divine act of salvation was required to give them everlasting life. Adam would have had everlasting life through eating the fruit of the tree of life, but as soon as he ate of the fruit of the tree of knowledge of good and evil, he forfeited his immortality. As Hobbes says in *Leviathan* chapter 38 (CL 301):

> We read that Adam was created in such a condition that, as long as he did not violate God's command, he could have lived to eternity in Paradise, where God had placed him. For in Paradise there was the *tree of life*, whose fruit he was allowed to eat as long as he abstained from eating the fruit of the tree of knowledge of good and evil. Therefore as soon as he ate of the forbidden fruit of this tree, God expelled him from Paradise (Genesis 3.22–23), *in case he put out his hand and ate the fruit of the tree of life, and lived to eternity*. So it is clear that Adam was not created immortal by virtue of his nature, but by the grace of God, namely by virtue of the *tree of life*, which prevented him from dying as long as he had a supply of its fruit to eat. It seems, then, as though, if Adam had not sinned, he would have lived in Paradise on Earth to eternity. But by this first sin, he and his descendants became mortal . . .

Hobbes then argues, with sometimes rather strained interpretations of the Bible, that after the second coming, the eternal life of the saved will be on Earth. As he says in *Leviathan* chapter 38 (CL 302):

> As for the place where people will enjoy this eternal life, these two texts from Scripture seem to indicate that this place will be

on Earth. For since Adam lost Paradise, and hence eternal life, Christ will restore the same Paradise and eternal life to those who believe in him, and not a different one.

Hobbes recognizes that there is a heaven, but it is God's throne, and not where humans will spend eternal life. As he says in the English *Leviathan* chapter 38 (CL 313):

> . . . the throne of this our great king [God] is in heaven, whereas the earth is only his footstool. It does not seem appropriate to the dignity of a king that the subjects of God should have any place as high as his throne, or higher than his footstool; nor can I find any obvious text for it in Holy Scripture.

Hobbes is aware that there will be a space problem if the saved are allowed to procreate to eternity, so sex is one of the pleasures missing from the afterlife. He says in *Leviathan* chapter 38 (CL 303):

> Further, our Saviour said (Matthew 22.30): 'After the resurrection they neither marry nor are married, but they will be like the angels of God in heaven.' This description is similar to that of the *eternal life* we lost in Adam, as far as marriage is concerned. For if Adam and Eve had not sinned, they would have lived in that Paradise on Earth without offspring in perpetuity. For if immortals generated offspring as humans do now, after not too long a time people would have no room to stand.

But what happens to people between dying and being resurrected for the last judgment? Hobbes is absolutely clear that souls do not go to heaven or remain in some sort of limbo. People are just dead, and remain dead until the resurrection. As he says in *Leviathan* chapter 38 (CL 303):

> . . . faithful Christians have recovered *eternal life* through the death of Christ, yet they will die a natural death, and will remain dead for some time, namely until the resurrection.

He clarifies this further in the Appendix to *Leviathan*, chapter 3 (CL 544):

A. ... And dying they will remain dead, until, thanks to the remission of sins through the death of Christ, they will be given a new, eternal life at the general resurrection of the dead. And according to this doctrine, the immortal souls of the dead (whether pious or impious) do not exist at all until the day of judgment.

B. I have already explained my position on this matter fully enough. But I would add that I do not understand how anyone can be said to sin against the Christian faith if they believe in eternal life, and it is irrelevant whether they hold that it is received at creation or at redemption. Nor do I understand how it can be against Christian teaching or worship, since neither the Holy Scripture (which contains Christian doctrine) nor the liturgy (which contains Christian worship) make any mention at all of the expression 'immortal soul', whereas there is frequent reference to 'eternal life through Christ.'

As for what God *does* when resurrecting a body, he gives it life just as he did first time round. As he says in the Appendix to *Leviathan* chapter 1 (CL 506):

A. But it seems to me that there are two difficulties here. The first is this. Given that to be resurrected is to be brought to life again, how will a human being be brought to life again in the grave, unless their soul is added to their body – either coming down from heaven or some limbo in heaven, or coming up from hell or purgatory?

B. What? Cannot God, who turned humans from earth into living animals, bring them back to life after they have been dissolved into earth?

Finally, there is the question of what happens after the last judgment. Hobbes has very little to say about life in Paradise, apart from the absence of sex. But if Paradise is on Earth, then where is hell? For his day and age, Hobbes took a remarkably humane stance: hell simply does not exist, and there is no eternal damnation. After the resurrection and last judgment, sinners are subjected to a second death, and their punishment is loss of eternal life rather than eternal punishment. In *Leviathan* chapter 38, after quoting Biblical passages talking of weeping and gnashing of teeth, and inextinguishable fire, Hobbes says (CL 309):

All these passages mean 'pain' metaphorically, as arising from the fact that they [sinners] see others acquire the eternal happiness which they themselves have forfeited through their unbelief and disobedience. But since the happiness of others is envied only by those who suffer pain and disasters, the consequence is that they suffer bodily punishment, which also includes a *second death*. For although Holy Scripture affirms the resurrection, we never read that *eternal life* is promised to sinners.

So, the only eternal life is the pleasant one for the faithful, and there is no eternal suffering for the damned – they are merely put to death a second time. And this is as it should be for an all-merciful God. As Hobbes says in the Appendix to *Leviathan*, chapter 1 (CL 507):

If you cite the passages in which God threatens the wicked with eternal tortures, you will not be able to deduce from these passages that the souls of the wicked exist between the day of their death and the day of judgment, but only that they exist *after* the day of judgment. Besides, the fact that God is just means that you cannot deduce from his *threatening* the wicked with eternal tortures, that their tortures will in fact be eternal. For someone who fails to come up with goods which are due is unjust; but someone who fails to come up with evils or penalties which are due is not unjust, but merciful. Is it not all the more possible for God, who is infinitely merciful, to reduce the length and severity of deserved punishments without violence to his justice? Then the Scripture says (*Revelation* 20.14) 'Hell itself will be thrown into the lake of fire, which is the second death.' So it seems that the wicked will be resurrected for a second death.

Hobbes's views on religion were certainly unorthodox, and they caused him considerable grief in an age when heresy was still a capital offence. Although his interpretations of the Bible and creeds were sometimes implausible and one-sided, he made a sincere attempt to recapture the beliefs of early Christianity before it was (in his view) corrupted by Greek philosophy. He tried to rid religion of superstition, and his denial of eternal damnation shows him in the best possible light.

CHAPTER 7

HOBBES'S INFLUENCE

i. RELIGION AND POLITICAL PHILOSOPHY

Unlike other early modern philosophers, Hobbes was not the founder of an identifiable philosophical school or movement. There
were Cartesians, Lockeans, Leibnizians and Humeans; but, apart
from a few isolated individuals, there were no Hobbesians. There
was a philosophy called 'Hobbism', which was how Hobbes's philosophy was popularly conceived; but it was universally a term of
abuse, and virtually no-one would admit to being a 'Hobbist'.
Although he did have his protectors and admirers, they were
cautious about identifying with his views publicly; and this makes
it more difficult to trace his influence than would otherwise be
the case.

In the popular imagination, as well as among educated people
who ought to have known better, Hobbes was held to be an atheist
because of his materialism. Despite what he actually said in his
various writings, hardly anyone could conceive how it was possible
to believe in God, angels and immortality without believing in
immaterial substances. And at that time, atheism was virtually
unthinkable. Again, despite the fact that Hobbes was an exceptionally restrained and abstemious person, he was assumed to be a
libertine because he held that all our actions are determined by our
bodily passions, and that what is good or evil depends on the desires
and aversions of each individual.

In addition, Hobbes caused offence to many different interest groups. His preference for monarchy offended democrats; his anti-clericism offended the bishops and other clergy; his treating the bible as a human product to be interpreted in the light of its historical context offended theologians; his attacks on the universities (and on mathematicians in particular) offended academics; his attacks on freedom of speech offended liberals; his ridiculing both of Catholics and of spiritualist superstitions in the last part of *Leviathan* offended both Catholics and those who held that the natural realm was at least partly spiritual. And it was not simply that he attacked these interested groups, but that he did so in such style, and with such wit, and with such apparent reasonableness and logic. This just made his enemies even more furious.

So even if Hobbes was short of disciples, he certainly succeeded in stimulating an extraordinarily large number of publications which were wholly or partly devoted to refuting his theories and arguments (depending on what you include, it was certainly well over a hundred in England and abroad). As a measure of fame, or at least of notoriety, this is an impressive record. Nor should it be seen as an entirely negative influence, since Hobbes had succeeded in forcing a large number of people into a rational defence of their beliefs by presenting them with reasoned arguments to which they had to respond in kind. Examples of some of the more fanciful titles of attacks on his philosophy are my collateral ancestor Alexander Ross's *Leviathan drawn out with a Hook* (1653), John Wallis's *Due correction for Mr. Hobbes: or, Schoole discipline, for not saying his lessons right* (1656), John Bramhall's *Castigations of Mr. Hobbes* and *The Catching of the Leviathan* (1658) and John Dowel's *The Leviathan Heretical* (1683).

In England, Hobbes had at least two followers, neither of whom does him much credit, but whose stories illustrate the intensity of feelings against him. One was Daniel Scargill, a fellow of Corpus Christi College, Cambridge, who was expelled for atheism in 1668. The authorities forced him to publish a grovelling retraction, in which he confessed to having been a Hobbist and an atheist, and to have indulged in all sorts of licentious behaviour. Despite the retraction, he was not reinstated, and he passed the rest of his life in impoverished obscurity. The other follower was the notorious poet, wit and libertine, the Earl of Rochester (1647–1680). As he was dying of venereal disease, he was counselled by the anti-Hobbesian bishop, Gilbert Burnet. As a result, he renounced his former life, and blamed it all on the 'absurd and foolish philosophy' of Hobbes. However, in neither case is there any historical evidence that they were actual followers of Hobbes, let alone that they were persuaded into atheism or licentiousness by his writings. It was just that Hobbes was a whipping-boy for any outrageous beliefs or behaviour.

While English publications about Hobbes were uniformly hostile, his political and religious ideas had a somewhat warmer reception on the Continent. Many of his works were readily available. His first philosophical publication, his objections to Descartes' *Meditations*, was published in France, and the Latin *On the Citizen* went through many editions, all printed in various countries on the Continent. Then virtually all his Latin writings, including the specially prepared translation of *Leviathan*, were published in Amsterdam in 1668, and reprinted in 1670. In addition, some of his writings were translated into various modern European languages. Because Hobbes was prohibited from publishing anything to do with religion in England, it is fair to say that the Continentals had easier access to his ideas than the English. Nevertheless, they too had their problems, with Hobbes's works being put on the Vatican's index of prohibited books, and at various times also being banned in Protestant countries such as Holland and Switzerland. But these bans had the unintended consequence of increasing demand for Hobbes's works, and it was sometimes noted that they fetched very high prices because of their scarcity.

As in England, there were many publications expressing horror at Hobbes's opinions. One common theme was a rejection of his thesis that, in a state of nature, everyone would be at war against everyone else. This was objectionable because, as Aristotle had held, civil society is not against nature, but natural to human beings. But more generally he was seen as a materialist and amoral atheist.

With the publication of the *Tractatus Theologico-Philosophicus* of Benedict de Spinoza (1632–1677) in 1670, Hobbes was joined by an even more outrageous atheist in the eyes of many, and the two names became linked together in the popular demonology. How far Spinoza was actually influenced by Hobbes is difficult to assess. Certainly Spinoza possessed a copy of *On the citizen*, and he could have had access to Hobbes's other Latin works through the 1668 edition, printed in Amsterdam. Certainly too there are resemblances between their ideas: they both rejected any form of superstition; they both treated the Bible as a human product; they both speculated about the origins of society; they both gave naturalistic accounts of ethics; they were both determinists and they both at least tended towards pantheism. No doubt Spinoza took comfort from the existence of a like-minded thinker, but there is little evidence of direct influence, and the differences are as striking as the resemblances. In religion, Spinoza held that the material world and the immaterial world of thought were two parallel aspects of God, whereas Hobbes reduced everything to body. In politics, Spinoza was a democrat and a champion of free speech, whereas Hobbes was a monarchist who believed that public speech should be censored. Spinoza simply was not a Hobbesian.

Towards the end of the seventh and into the eighteenth century, there was a growing anti-religious literature, much of it anonymous. Just as Hobbes and Spinoza were demonized by conservative writers, they were hailed as prophets of enlightenment by these free-thinkers. For them, what mattered about Hobbes and Spinoza was their supposed atheism and their revisionist interpretations of the Bible. This movement culminated in the rational secularism of the French encyclopaedists in the middle of the eighteenth century, and the explicit atheism of Baron d'Holbach (1723–1789).

By contrast, there were other, more moderate writers who were strongly attracted by Hobbes's political ideas, but rejected his religious views as too extreme. An interesting early example is that of a couple of Cartesians (Jacques du Roure and Pierre-Sylvan Regis) who wrote treatises on philosophy relying mainly on Descartes, but drawing heavily on Hobbes's *On the Citizen* for political philosophy. It is interesting, because Hobbes and Descartes were extremely hostile to each other. The reason why Hobbes's work was used is probably because Descartes did not write about political philosophy, and, despite their differences, both were seen as leading lights of the modern philosophy which the Cartesians hoped would replace traditional scholasticism.

So far the case for Hobbes's influence on political philosophy has been somewhat mixed. But there are two fundamental concepts to which his major contribution cannot be denied. The first is that of the social contract, of which he was the main inventor. Although it was adapted in different ways by later philosophers, it was central to the political philosophy of John Locke (1632–1704), whose ideas had a profound influence on the constitution of the United States. It was also a fundamental component of the philosophy of Jean Jacques Rousseau (1712–1778), and it has been revived in recent times by philosophers such as John Rawls (1921–2002).

The second concept is that of natural law. Although the concept was not original to Hobbes, he developed it in a unique way, which was highly influential on the great seventeenth-century philosopher of law, Samuel Pufendorf (1632–1694), and again on John Locke. As with the concept of a social contract, that of natural law is still very much a live issue, with modern proponents such as John Finnis (1940–).

ii. METAPHYSICS

While Hobbes was in exile in France, he was an active member of the Mersenne circle, and he was widely respected as one of the leading lights of the modern movement, as much for his science and metaphysics as for his political philosophy. He was generally regarded as one of the top half-dozen or so philosophers, along with Galileo, Descartes, Gassendi and a few others. He retained the respect of his former colleagues long after his return to England, but there is no evidence of his having had any influence on the development of French philosophy, which was dominated by reverence for his opponent Descartes. Indeed, his metaphysics seems to have had no direct influence on anyone or significance, with the one major exception of Gottfried Wilhelm Leibniz (1646–1716).

That Hobbes influenced Leibniz may seem surprising, because Leibniz's philosophy was based on the idea that the ultimate components of reality were immaterial, spiritual substances – quite the opposite of Hobbes's body. But in his youth, Leibniz had a brief dalliance with materialist philosophy, and he was an avid reader and admirer of Hobbes's works. He carefully studied the 1668 edition of Hobbes's Latin works, as well as individual books that had been published earlier. He wrote a long and flattering letter to Hobbes in 1670, to which he got no reply, and another in about 1674, which also remained unanswered.

It is hard to disentangle precisely how much Leibniz owed to Hobbes, because many aspects of the new mechanical philosophy were common to all the leading moderns, who Leibniz listed as 'Galileo, Bacon, Gassendi, Descartes, Hobbes, and Digby'. He could have acquired the basic principles of the new philosophy from any or all of them. However, there are a number of distinctive ideas which Leibniz could only have got from Hobbes, and which survived (though with substantial modifications) into his mature philosophy.

The first of these is Hobbes's theory that all reasoning is a form of computation, or the addition and subtraction of names which have been given strict definitions. Leibniz built on this to develop his ambitious but unfulfilled programme for a 'universal characteristic'. Like Hobbes before him, Leibniz devoted an immense amount of time to producing lists of definitions of key concepts in a wide range of disciplines. His ultimate goal was to replace verbal definitions with a numerical code which would specify the logical relations between concepts of different levels of generality. For example, the code for 'human being' would make it explicit that it is what is produced by adding the concept of 'rational' to the concept of 'animal'. Reasonings are valid only if they consist in making explicit what is already contained in concepts; but in ordinary language, the definitions of concepts are disputed, and arguments remain unresolved because of lack of agreement on definitions. Leibniz's vision, inspired by Hobbes, was that it should be possible to create a dictionary of all possible concepts, notated in such a way that there would be no place for interminable arguments, but instead the logical consequences could be calculated arithmetically. As Leibniz said in an undated note (*Philosophischen Schriften* VII, 200):

But to return to the expression of thoughts by means of characters, I thus think that controversies can never be resolved, nor
sectarian disputes be silenced, unless we renounce complicated
chains of reasoning in favour of simple *calculations*, and vague
terms of uncertain meaning in favour of determinate *characters*.
In other words, it must be brought about that every fallacy
becomes nothing other than a *calculating error*, and every *soph-
ism* expressed in this new type of notation becomes in fact
nothing other than a *grammatical* or *linguistic error*, easily
proved to be such by the very laws of this philosophical gram-
mar. Once this has been achieved, when controversies arise, there
will be no more need for a disputation between two philosophers
than there would be between two accountants. It would be
enough for them to pick up their pens and sit at their abacuses,
and say to each other (perhaps having summoned a mutual
friend): 'Let us calculate.'

Leibniz actually designed and had constructed a calculating
machine, which could be regarded as a prototype for the modern
computer. His vision was no more than an extension of Hobbes's
belief that all scientific reasoning should be as definitive and inar-
guable as geometry already was.

The second idea Leibniz may have got from Hobbes was that all
truth is analytic. In *On body* chapter 3 section 7, Hobbes wrote:

A *true* proposition is one in which the *predicate* contains the
subject, or in which the *predicate* is the name of everything of
which the *subject* is the name. For example, 'A human is an
animal' is a true proposition because whatever is called 'human'
is also called 'animal'. And 'Some human is sick' is true, since
'sick' is the name of some human. A proposition is called *false*
if it is not true, or if its *predicate* does not include its *subject*; for
example 'A human is a stone.'

This is almost identical to Leibniz's oft-repeated assertion that in
every true proposition, the concept of the predicate is contained in
the concept of the subject. The one big difference is that, whereas

for Leibniz the predicate is contained in the subject, for Hobbes it is the other way round. However, they are not contradicting each other, because Hobbes's definition is *extensional*, and Leibniz's is *intensional*. In other words, Hobbes is saying that the predicate has a wider scope or extension than the subject. Everything that is included in the subject is also included in the predicate, and there are things that are included in the predicate, but not in the subject. For example, all things to which the name 'human being' applies are animals, but not all animals are human beings. Leibniz, on the other hand, defines truth in terms of the meaning or intension of concepts. So, given that the concept of a human being is that of a rational animal, the concept of the predicate 'animal' is contained in the concept of the subject 'human being'. The reason for the difference is that Hobbes was a nominalist, who held that only things and names existed, and therefore could not define truth in terms of concepts. Whereas Leibniz was a realist, who held that concepts existed in their own right, and were indeed logically prior to individual existents.

A third way in which Leibniz may have been influenced by Hobbes is a rather curious one. In Chapter 2 section vi, we saw how Hobbes held that, although our senses are constantly being bombarded by vibrations in the ether and the air, we have only one conscious sensation at a time. He thus distinguished between conscious sensations, and the myriads of phantasms that are generated every time an incoming conation is met by an outgoing equal and opposite conation. And presumably this is true, not merely of sense organs, but of any interaction between bodies. As Hobbes says in *On Body* chapter 25 section 5:

> Even though, as I have said, all sensation occurs by reaction, it is not necessarily the case that whatever reacts has a sensation. I know there have been philosophers, and learned ones at that, who have held that all bodies were endowed with sensation; nor do I see how they could be refuted, if the nature of sensation consisted in reaction alone. But even if bodies other than sentient ones had some sort of phantasm whenever they reacted, it would cease as soon as the object went away. Unless they had

organs capable of retaining an impressed motion even after the object had gone away, as animals have, their sensation would be unaccompanied by any memory that they had sensed – and this has nothing to do with the sort of sensation we are talking about here.

Although he does not go along with the vitalists, who held that everything was full of life and sensation, he comes close to it with his suggestion that phantasms are generated everywhere. As a thoroughgoing monist (someone who believes there is only one kind of substance), Hobbes was compelled to account for all the phenomena of nature with the same basic concepts. So, although he accepted the commonsense distinction between three kinds of being: inanimate objects, animals and human beings, he had to account for the capacities of the higher-order beings as due to the same forces that characterized the simplest ones. So, if a phantasm is generated when, say, light strikes the eye of an animal and meets with an equal and opposite reaction, the same must be true of a collision between two inanimate objects. Where animals (including humans) differ from inanimate objects is that they have conscious *sensations* as well as phantasms, and these sensations are possible because animals can remember their sensations from one moment to the next, and compare them with each other. If a phantasm came and went in an instant without being remembered, there would be no consciousness of it. As for the difference between human and animal sensations, as we saw in Chapter 3 section iv above, this consists in the fact that humans can add a verbal running commentary to what they perceive.

Leibniz was also a monist, but a spiritualist one. So, although his philosophy might seem to be diametrically opposed to Hobbes's, he had precisely the same need to explain the three levels of being with the same basic concepts. He held that the universe consisted of an infinity of 'monads', or immaterial, spiritual atoms, characterized by perception and conation. In the lowest order of monads, there was no consciousness at all. In monads constituting the souls of animals, perception was accompanied by memory, thus yielding conscious sensations. And humans were distinguished from other animals, not by the possession of language, as Hobbes held, but by self-consciousness, so that only humans are aware of themselves as having conscious sensations. As he said in his early *Theory of Abstract Motion* of 1671 (*Philosophischen Schriften* IV.230):

> *No conation which does not result in motion lasts more than an instant, except in minds.* For what happens at an instant is a conation, whereas what happens over time is the motion of a body. This opens the door for discovering the real difference between body and mind, which no-one has yet explained. For every body is a momentary mind, or a mind that lacks *memory*, because it does not retain its own conation together with the contrary conation of another body beyond an instant. But two things are required for there to be *sensation*, namely action and reaction, or in other words comparison, and hence *harmony* – and also *pleasure* or pain, without which there is no sensation. So a body lacks memory; it lacks any sensation of its actions and passions; and it lacks thought.

Finally, this brings us to by far the most significant way in which Hobbes influenced Leibniz, namely through the concept of conation, which we looked at in Chapter 3 section xi above. Leibniz wrote the *Theory of Abstract Motion* before he had developed his mature, spiritualist metaphysics, and while he was most heavily influenced by Hobbes, and especially by his concept of conation and infinitesimal quantities in general. Although he diverges from Hobbes on points of detail, his broad position is that the smallest components of the material world are infinitesimals; that they are endowed with conations which are infinitesimal motions; that conations are propagated to infinity in the plenum; that a given body is subject to a multiplicity of conations at one and the same time; and that nothing is absolutely at rest. Although Leibniz's mature philosophy is of course different, there was a smooth transition from this Hobbesian material world to Leibniz's later world of an infinity of immaterial monads whose perceptions and conations are in perfect harmony with each other.

But even more important than the influence of Hobbes's concept of conation on Leibniz's metaphysics was its influence on his mathematics. It was the key concept that led to Leibniz's discovery of the infinitesimal calculus, and raised mathematics to an entirely new level. Hobbes may have been a far weaker mathematician than he prided himself on being, but he laid the foundations for others greater than himself.

iii. CONCLUSION

As I hope this book has succeeded in showing, Hobbes was one of the leaders of the modern movement in philosophy and science, and his political philosophy was only one string to his bow. He was certainly recognized as one of the greats by intellectuals on the Continent. On returning to England after his exile in France, he must have looked back at this period of respect and intellectual cooperation with nostalgia, given his demonization as an atheist and amoralist, and his bitter feuds with mathematicians and bishops.

Hobbes may have achieved the lasting fame he desired, but certainly not in the way he had hoped. His mathematical writings were an embarrassment, and his failure to acknowledge his mistakes did much to fuel opposition to the rest of his work. With the sole exception of Leibniz, his philosophical system had little impact on the subsequent development of philosophy or science, either in England or on the Continent. Although he anticipated advances which would take place much later – especially linguistic philosophy and materialist psychology – there is no evidence of his having had any direct influence. And even in political science, of which he believed he himself was the founder, his theories have generally been taken as an interesting extreme position to be avoided, rather than as an example to be followed. It is a sad fact that, although *Leviathan* is a must for any course on politics, Hobbes's metaphysical writings are conspicuous by their absence from most courses on the history of modern philosophy.

The key to Hobbes's peculiar mix of success and failure is a sign of the times to which he belonged. Along with most of the other leaders of the modern revolution, he was not an academic, and he by-passed the control systems which prevented egregious rubbish from being published, but at the same time stifled new and unconventional ideas. If the universities of the seventeenth century had had the same monopoly over research that they have in the twenty-first century, the works of Hobbes, Descartes, Spinoza, Leibniz and other non-academics would never have seen the light of day. They could think outside the box, because they were not inside the box; but the downside was that there was no-one between them and their printers to prevent them from making fools of themselves with half-baked ideas that had not been reviewed by their peers. Hobbes had an exceptionally fertile intellectual imagination, which gave rise to some of the most exciting ideas in modern thought. He knew that he was breaking new intellectual ground, and that he had nothing to learn from the universities, at least as they were when he was a student. But he was over-confident, and in the case of mathematics at least, he failed to appreciate the advances that had been made in his own lifetime. His reputation would have been better if he had been dissuaded from publishing his supposed proofs of squaring the circle, and his attacks on university mathematics.

But Hobbes was a great, independent thinker, and perhaps the best evidence of his greatness is that his name is still a household word, whereas even most of today's university philosophers would struggle to name anyone who was a university philosopher in Hobbes's time.

SOURCES

i. HOBBES TEXTS

The main sources for Hobbes texts are the monumental, if somewhat defective editions by William Molesworth:

The English Works, 11 volumes (London, Bohn, 1839–1845) = EW.
Opera philosophica quæ latine scripsit omnia, 5 volumes (London, Bohn, 1839–1845) = OL.

Since then there have been some proper scholarly editions of individual works, but not as many as one would expect for one of the greatest English philosophers. The editions I have used for my translations are:

An Answer to Dr. Bramhall, EW, volume 4.
N. Malcolm (ed.) (1994), *The Correspondence of Thomas Hobbes*. Oxford: Clarendon Press, 2 volumes.
J. C. A. Gaskin (ed.) (1994), *The Elements of Law*. Oxford: Oxford University Press.
Leviathan (Latin), OL, volume 3.
E. Curley (ed.) (1994), *Leviathan* (English). Indianapolis: Hackett.
Objections to Descartes' *Meditations*, in C. Adam and P. Tannery (eds) (1897–1910), *Oeuvres de Descartes*. Paris: Le Cerf, volume 7, pp. 171–196.
Of Liberty and Necessity, EW, volume 4.
On Body: De corpore, OL, volume 1.
On Body (anonymous contemporary English translation), EW, volume 1.
On the Human Being: De homine, OL, volume 2.
The Questions concerning Liberty, Necessity and Chance, EW, volume 5.
Ten Dialogues of Natural Philosophy, EW, volume 7.

ii. OTHER PRIMARY TEXTS

Anselm (1931), *On Faith in the Trinity and on the Incarnation of the Word, against the Blasphemies of Roscelin: De fide trinitatis et de incarnatione verbi contra blasphemias Roscelini*, in *Recherches de Théologie Ancienne et Médiévale*. Louvain: Abbaye du Mont César, volume 3.

Carroll, Lewis (1939), *The Complete Works*. London: The Nonesuch Press.

Descartes (1897–1910), *Discourse on the Method: Discours de la méthode*, in C. Adam and P. Tannery (eds), *Oeuvres de Descartes*. Paris: Le Cerf, volume 6.

Descartes, *Meditations on First Philosophy: Meditationes de prima philosophia*, Adam and Tannery, volume 7.

Descartes, *Treatise on the Human Being: Traité de l'homme*, Adam and Tannery, volume 11.

Descartes, *The World, or Treatise on Light: Le monde, ou, traité de la lumière*, Adam and Tannery, volume 11.

Galileo (1623), *The Assayer: Il saggiatore*. Rome: Mascardi.

Leibniz (1875–1890), C. I. Gerhardt (ed.), *Die philosophischen Schriften* Berlin: Weidmann, 7 volumes.

Plato (1961), H. N. Fowler (ed.) *Theaetetus and Sophist*. London: Heinemann.

Plato (1929), R.G. Bury (ed.), *Timaeus*. London: Heinemann.

iii. HOBBES'S BIOGRAPHY

Hobbes, *Vita*, and *Vita carmine expessa*, OL, volume 1.

Aubrey, John (1982), 'Hobbes', in R. Barber (ed.), *Brief Lives*. Woodbridge: Boydell, pp. 148–162.

Malcolm, Noel (1996), 'A summary biography of Hobbes', in T. Sorell (ed.), *The Cambridge Companion to Hobbes*. Cambridge: Cambridge University Press, pp. 13–44.

Martinich, A. P. (1999), *Hobbes: A Biography*. Cambridge, Cambridge University Press.

Malcolm, Noel (2004), 'Hobbes', in H.C.G. Matthew and B. Harrison (eds), *Oxford Dictionary of National Biography*. Oxford: Oxford University Press.

iv. HOBBES'S INFLUENCE

MacDonald, Ross George (2007), 'Leibniz's debt to Hobbes', in P. Phemister and S. Brown, (eds), *Leibniz and the English-Speaking World*. Dordrecht: Springer, pp. 19–33.

SOURCES

Mintz, Samuel I. (1962), *The Hunting of Leviathan*. Cambridge: Cambridge University Press.

Malcolm, Noel (2002), 'Hobbes and the European Republic of Letters', *Aspects of Hobbes*. Oxford: Clarendon Press, pp. 457–545.

CONTINUING WITH HOBBES

After reading this short introduction, I hope you will want to study Hobbes in greater depth. It is always a good idea to read a philosopher's own writings, and I would recommend starting with *The Elements of Law*, which is Hobbes's most approachable work. Then you can try *Leviathan*, especially the first two parts, which cover all the essentials of his metaphysics and political philosophy. You might find it helpful to read *Leviathan* in conjunction with Glen Newey, *Routledge philosophy guidebook to Hobbes and Leviathan* (London, Routledge, 2008).

In case you find Hobbes's English difficult, I have translated large parts of the above works (and more besides) into modern English, and I have made them freely available at the following website:

http://www.philosophy.leeds.ac.uk/GMR/hmp/texts/modern/hobbes/
hobbesindex.html.

The following is a selection of books that discuss Hobbes's philosophy in greater detail than has been possible in this short introduction:

Malcolm, Noel (2002), *Aspects of Hobbes*. Oxford: Clarendon Press.
Oakeshott, Michael (1975), *Hobbes on Civil Association*. Oxford: Blackwell.
Peters, Richard (1956), *Hobbes*. Harmondsworth: Penguin.
Pettit, Philip (2008), *Made with Words: Hobbes on Language, Mind, and Politics*. Princeton: Princeton University Press.
Raphael, David (1977), *Hobbes: Morals and Politics*. London: Allen and Unwin.
G. A. J. Rogers and Alan Ryan (eds), *Perspectives on Thomas Hobbes*. Oxford: Clarendon Press.
Quentin Skinner (1996), *Reason and Rhetoric in the Philosophy of Hobbes*. Cambridge: Cambridge University Press.

Sorell, Tom (1986), *Hobbes*. London: Routledge.

Sorell, Tom (ed.) (1996), *The Cambridge Companion to Hobbes*. Cambridge: Cambridge University Press.

Strauss, Leo (1936), *The Political Philosophy of Hobbes: Its Basis and its Genesis*. Tr. Elsa Sinclair. Oxford: Clarendon Press.

Warrender, Howard (1957), *The Political Philosophy of Hobbes: His Theory of Obligation*. Oxford: Clarendon Press.

Watkins, John (1973), *Hobbes's System of Ideas: A Study in the Political Significance of Philosophical Theories* (2nd edn). London: Hutchinson.

Wright, George (2005), *Religion, Politics, and Thomas Hobbes*. Dordrecht: Springer.

INDEX

On the Human Being 1, 10, 14, 36, 53, 88, 90, 97
Optical Treatise 10, 25, 39, 88

pain 28–9, 91, 97–8, 155, 159, 170
peace 105, 106–9, 129–33
perception, theories of 18–24
person 114–15
phantasm, phantasy 26–31, 34, 47, 49, 65, 81, 89–90, 140, 168–9
Plato 27, 30, 38, 53, 60–1, 72, 76, 94, 114, 155
pleasure 28–9, 97–8, 155, 170
point 82–3
political philosophy 36, 110–14
possibility 84–6
pushing and pulling 24–5, 79–80
Pythagoras 72

qualities, primary and secondary 19–23, 29–33
Questions concerning Liberty 99

realism 59–61
reason 21, 32–5, 42–3, 51, 64, 101, 106, 108, 143, 166–7
right of nature 107–8
Rochester, Earl of 163
Roscelin, Jean 62
Royal Society 14, 59

Sadducees 149
Sarpi, Pietro 8
Scargill, Daniel 162
science 33–7, 59, 110–11
sensation 27, 29–30, 89, 168–70
social contract 114–20, 128–9, 165
Socrates 118
solidity 32

soul 26, 28, 37, 51–6, 60, 90, 92–4, 100, 149, 155–9
sovereign 111–22, 123–38
space 31–3, 69–71
species 18–19, 22–4
Spinoza, Benedict de 151, 163–4
spirit 26, 50–3, 135, 143, 150–5, 169–70
squaring the circle 15, 72–4, 172
state 35–6, 111–16
Stoic philosophy 20, 151
Suárez, Francisco de 45
substance 19, 32, 48–53, 135, 138, 140, 149–50
summum bonum 92–3
sun 21, 27–8, 33, 79–80

Ten Dialogues 16, 81, 153
Tertullian 149, 152
Torricelli, Evangelista 57
truth 66–8, 167–8

unconscious, the 27, 90
universals 38, 59–66
universities 14, 23–4, 43–4, 73, 131–3, 139, 172

vacuum 15, 56–9, 153
Viète, François 74–5
visual stream 27

Wallis, John 15, 162
war 103–6, 127, 129
Warner, Walter 9
White, Thomas 11–12
will 93–6
witches 51
Wittgenstein, Ludwig 44, 142